I0796911

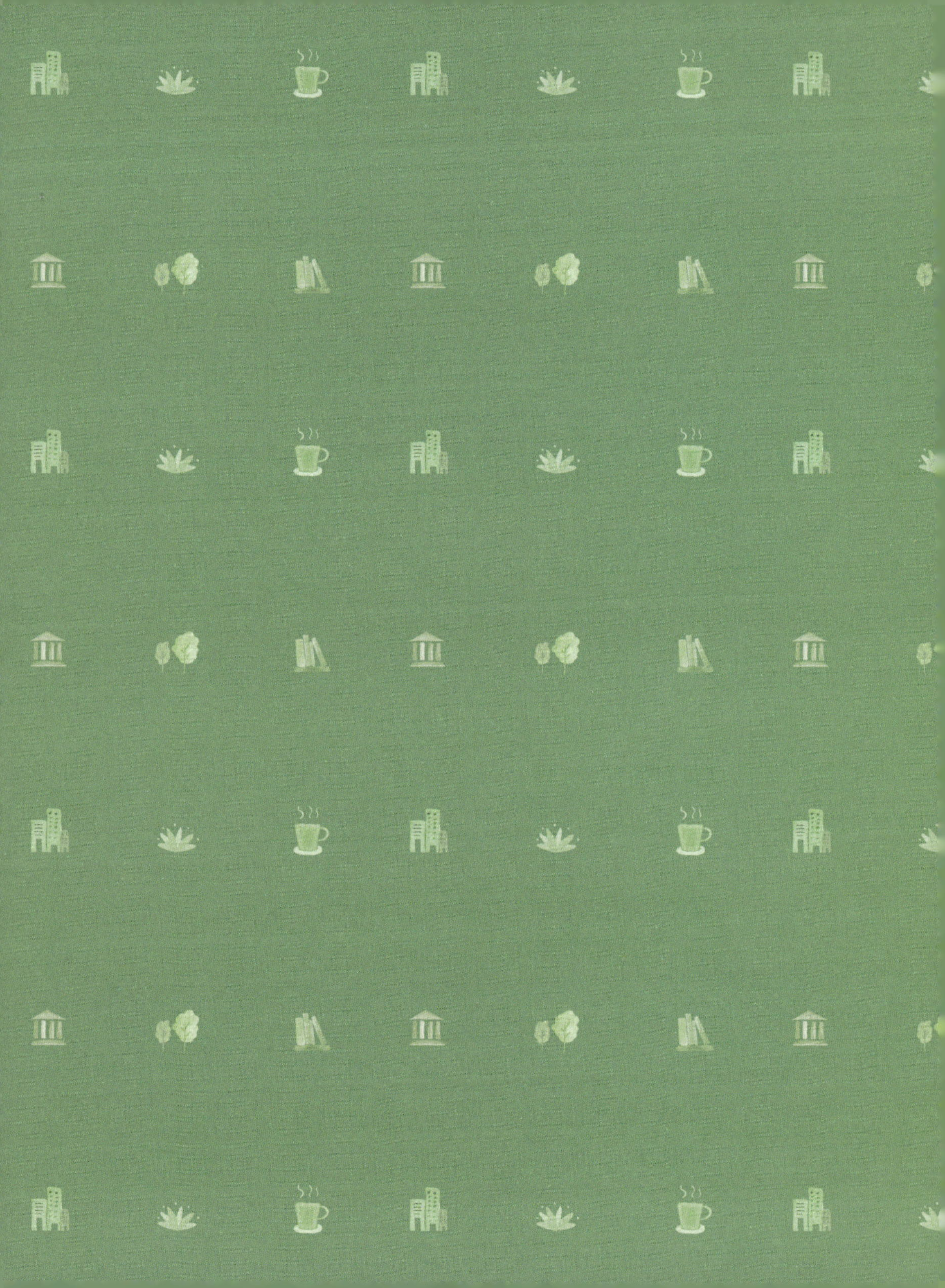

Quietest Places *in* New York City

Finding Calm & Peace in Urban Chaos

Nicole Kelner

Rizzoli Universe

Contents

BROOKLYN
Tea

Introduction

From honking cars to screaming sirens, New York City plays a soundtrack that never stops. I often feel like a treasure hunter, searching for quiet moments in one of the loudest places on Earth. But within its five boroughs there are hidden pockets of peace. This book is here to help you find quiet, around you and within you.

Over the past seven years, I have lived in six different neighborhoods and three boroughs in New York, and spent a lot of time discovering secret gardens, rooftop farms, waterfall parks, and charming cafes that have become my city sanctuaries. I have designed mindfulness practices inspired by each location to help you cultivate not only external stillness but an internal calm.

As an artist focused on watercolor paintings about climate solutions, I approached this book through a similar lens. Nearly half of the places I share are green spaces. Most of the restaurants are plant-based or farm-to-table. And I have uncovered creative ways New York is becoming more climate-resilient.

It is said that noise is like the canary in the coal mine of climate change. During my time as artist-in-residence at a nonprofit called Quiet Communities, its president, Dr. Jamie Banks, helped me understand that noise is often created by fossil-fuel-powered machines, like cars, planes, and leaf blowers. This noise pollution sounds an alarm that our world is out of balance.

As I listened more closely, I realized that while fossil fuels are noisy, renewable energy is quiet. I hope these pages help you imagine a quieter, more sustainable future–one where cities are more walkable, filled with protected bike lanes and open streets. Picture electric cars gliding down the Brooklyn-Queens Expressway and apartments powered by heat pumps instead of humming air conditioners. Imagine a New York with lush green spaces that provide shade, buffer noise, and support thriving ecosystems for birds and wildlife. Across the country, we could build efficient public transportation, replacing short-haul flights with high-speed trains. I like to envision a world where people can sleep more soundly, experience less stress, and have healthier hearts and minds.

Quiet is not the absence of sound, it is the presence of calm, both external and internal. You might be sitting in a silent room at the Brooklyn Public Library yet be overwhelmed by your thoughts. Conversely, you might be standing in the middle of Times Square and feel surprisingly serene.

With pinging emails and pop-up notifications pulling at our attention, people travel across the world or go to silent retreats in search of peace. I've been one of those people. I once traveled abroad to a remote monastery and spent weeks meditating. But when I returned to New York, I realized that serenity is possible here too. So, I combed through my two thousand stars on Google Maps, distilled ten years of meditation practice, and created this bucket-list guide to finding calm in the city. I've curated sixty-seven of my favorite places and designed custom itineraries for restorative day trips. I hope this book reveals that quiet can be just a subway ride away.

This is my official invitation to take out your AirPods and go offline as you visit each of these special spaces. Turning down the digital noise is a powerful tool to settle our minds, which helps us hear and see more clearly. Through this mindset, you can enter a world of wonder and presence, allowing you to discover the quietest places in New York City.

Sometimes I worry that by sharing these places they will no longer be quiet. But I hope that by celebrating them, we can protect and preserve them. Visiting when they are empty is wonderful, but being quiet together is magical too.

Finding quiet has been essential for my mental health and well-being. The mindfulness practices in this book are inspired by Buddhist philosophy, somatic exercises, cognitive behavioral therapy, and forest bathing. Each prompt is shaped by the landscape or architecture of its location, working in harmony with the environment to deepen your connection to the city.

For me, quiet is sitting by the pond in Green-Wood Cemetery, listening to the wild parakeets chirp at sunset. It is picking up pebbles on Brighton Beach in January and hearing waves wash against the shore. It is walking through Prospect Park during off-leash hours, watching dogs joyfully run free. It is drawing in my sketchbook on Governors Island, getting lost in my art. In these moments, time slows down.

I don't believe silence is golden but that quiet is like gold: it is rare, valuable, and luxurious. Let this book be inspiration for you to uncover pockets of peace hiding in New York. I've created a map, but I hope this is just the start of your own quiet adventure.

1. Albertine
2. Brooklyn Public Library
3. Center for Brooklyn History
4. The Center for Fiction
5. Community Bookstore
6. Housing Works Bookstore
7. Jefferson Market Library
8. L'Alliance New York
9. The Morgan Library
10. Poets House
11. Rose Main Reading Room at the NYPL

Libraries & Bookstores

"Flow" is a mental state where you're fully immersed in what you're doing and time seems to disappear. While at a library, lose yourself in a book and let the world fade away.

Albertine

972 FIFTH AVENUE IN MANHATTAN
(between 78th and 79th Streets)

As you step through the marble-floored lobby of the Payne Whitney mansion, you're transported to the Gilded Age. The Venetian Room greets you with ornately framed art and floor-to-ceiling mirrors—a mini-Versailles on the Upper East Side. As you climb the grand staircase, you'll arrive at Albertine, a hidden French bookstore.

When I first walked into Albertine, I fell in love with the royal blue hand-painted mural on the ceiling, featuring constellations, stars, and planets and modeled after the music room at the Villa Stuck in Munich, Germany.

As you sit on the oversize leather couch, gaze up at the stars painted on the ceiling. Think back to a time when you were stargazing outside. While you reminisce about a place where the night sky was dark and illuminated by a sea of stars, allow a gentle smile to come across your face. This is a reminder that you can find joy anytime, simply by recalling a beautiful memory.

Recommendations: 1. Read in the backyard in the Florence Gould Garden. 2. Pop over to the Isle of Us for a quick, healthy brunch. 3. Wander toward the Central Park Boathouse for lunch by the lake.

Brooklyn Public Library

10 GRAND ARMY PLAZA IN BROOKLYN
(between Eastern Parkway and Flatbush Avenue)

The Brooklyn Public Library's Central Branch looks more like a museum than a neighborhood library. As you pass through the Corinthian-style pillars and the thirty-foot bronze doors, you are welcomed into a sanctuary of books. The doors are lined with fifteen bronze panels depicting scenes from iconic American literature, such as *Moby Dick*, *Tom Sawyer*, and *The Raven*.

Officially known as the Central Library, this Art Deco landmark is home to over a million books and serves as a cultural hub for the city. With exhibitions, author talks, and creative programs filling its calendar year-round, it is a powerhouse of the public library system.

Bring a journal and write down what quiet means to you. Quiet often appears in the transition from a loud place to a less noisy space. Where have you found these pockets of calm in the city or around the world? Reflect on what activities or places give you the most calm and peace as you write your own list of quiet places.

Recommendations: 1. Borrow a book and read in the wetlands by the Prospect Park boathouse. 2. Shop at the Grand Army Plaza Greenmarket for fresh produce and flowers on a Saturday. 3. Head over to the nearby Brooklyn Museum to enjoy an art-filled afternoon.

Center for Brooklyn History

128 PIERREPONT STREET IN BROOKLYN

(between Henry and Clinton Streets)

My favorite library in New York is tucked inside the second floor of the Center for Brooklyn History. As you walk into the Othmer Library, you're welcomed into a reading room with spiral staircases, stained-glass windows, and mahogany tables.

This Romanesque Revival building in Brooklyn Heights was constructed in 1863 as the Brooklyn Historical Society. In 2020, it merged with the Brooklyn Public Library to become the Center for Brooklyn History.

It is the only library I know of where you are personally greeted and asked to check your bag in a cubby. While laptops and notebooks are welcome, the simple act of leaving your belongings at the door creates a sense of separation from the outside world, allowing you to tune in to your internal world.

Pause and rest your hands on the table, palms facing up. Notice how they are almost always in motion, whether texting, gripping a subway pole, or carrying a coffee. Look at the lines on your palms, the swirls of your fingerprints, and the texture of your skin. Feel gratitude for all that they allow you to do.

Recommendations: 1. Go for a walk through two lovely neighborhoods, Cobble Hill and Carroll Gardens. Get coffee at Saturn Road while sipping on it in the beautiful backyard. 2. Grab a pastry from Mazzola and enjoy it in The Secret Garden Brooklyn. 3. Drop in for a writing class or community group at Brooklyn Poets.

The Center for Fiction

15 LAFAYETTE AVENUE IN BROOKLYN
(between Rockwell and Ashland Places)

In Downtown Brooklyn, the Center for Fiction is more than a bookstore: it is a writer's studio, literary event space, and cafe. The first floor is lined with floor-to-ceiling shelves of fiction. But one of the best-kept secrets is the membership, which grants you access to a hidden second floor. Members can access a private lounge, a tech-free reading room, an outdoor terrace, and borrowing privileges from a library of seventy thousand books. If you're just visiting, the Center offers day passes for a relaxing afternoon in the members' lounge.

Founded in 1821 in Manhattan as the Mercantile Library of New York, it was once the largest lending library in the country. Today, it serves as a literary nonprofit celebrating the art of fiction. They host writing workshops, author talks, and community events.

Bring a journal, grab a coffee downstairs, and reflect on your week in your notebook. Do a "Rose, Thorn, Bud" exercise: write down one joyful moment, a challenging moment, and an activity you're looking forward to. Instead of judging the highs or lows, see them as part of the tapestry of your life.

Recommendations: 1. Go on a book-lovers tour and support Greenlight Bookstore, a few blocks away. 2. Continue the tour at the new branch of the Brooklyn Public Library, the Library for Arts and Culture. 3. Go on a Saturday to pick up fresh produce for the week at the Fort Greene Park Greenmarket.

Community Bookstore

143 SEVENTH AVENUE IN BROOKLYN

(between Garfield Place and Carroll Street)

This Park Slope institution is Brooklyn's oldest independent bookstore. Its hidden gem is the tiny backyard patio enveloped in ivy-covered walls. Complete with a pond and a few little frogs, you can sneak away and get lost in a new book. I love going to the patio to read and hear the New York noise melt away.

The well-worn wooden floors create the sense that you're at a friend's apartment—but one filled with every book you want to read. Author readings and book clubs bring together local writers and creatives in a welcoming community space. If you're lucky, you may even meet the friendly cat, who is often perched among the titles. We've all heard of bodega cats, but we need more bookstore cats.

Sit by the pond and look at the black cherry tree. Imagine its roots stretching deep into the earth, connecting with the neighboring trees. Trees can communicate with one another, sending nutrients through an underground network of fungi. Picture this living ecosystem of mycelium and roots thriving just inches beneath your feet.

COMMUNITY
BOOKSTORE

Recommendations: 1. Head to Un Posto Italiano to pick up fresh pasta for dinner. 2. Cross the street and go to Electric Beets for a vegan lunch or power smoothie. Try the lasagna. 3. Stop by Winner in the Park for a breakfast sandwich and eat it by the Picnic House.

Housing Works Bookstore

126 CROSBY STREET IN MANHATTAN
(between Houston and Prince Streets)

In the heart of SoHo is a bookstore and cafe with a heartwarming goal. Housing Works's mission is to end the dual crises of HIV/AIDS and homelessness through providing housing and advocating for policy changes. It was founded in 1990 by four members of the AIDS activist group ACT UP: Keith Cylar, Charles King, Eric Sawyer, and Virginia Shubert. All the books are donated, and the cafe is run by volunteers, ensuring that 100 percent of the proceeds go directly to their nonprofit work.

I first came here for a poetry reading in the evening, sitting beneath a row of glowing lights as they illuminated the dark wooden bookcases. Housing Works hosts author talks, performances, and creative thrift shop events throughout the year to gather community.

After five p.m., the coffee shop becomes a laptop-free zone, inviting you to unplug in an analog atmosphere. Wander the shelves and pick up a book that grabs your attention. Open to a random page, read a sentence, and see if the words offer a message that resonates with you.

Recommendations: 1. Volunteer for a garden day with the Hudson River Park community. 2. Get dinner at LuAnne's Wild Ginger and try the general tsoy's seitan. 3. Hop on the F train to Carroll Gardens and continue on the bookshop cafe tour at Liz's Book Bar.

Jefferson Market Library

425 SIXTH AVENUE IN MANHATTAN

(between Christopher and West 10th Streets)

Standing tall in Greenwich Village, the Jefferson Market Library looks more like a Victorian Gothic clock tower than a public library. Originally built in the 1870s as a courthouse, this landmark building is filled with stained-glass windows and has a spiral staircase.

During its days as a courthouse, the basement held prisoners awaiting trial, a wild contrast to the reference rooms it holds today. Next door once stood the Women's House of Detention, Manhattan's only women's prison, which was demolished in the 1970s and transformed into the Jefferson Market Garden. Its rose-lined gates and native plants create the illusion you're far from the street, even though the city is just steps away.

Sit beside the koi pond and place one hand on your heart. As you breathe in deeply, acknowledge that the air contains oxygen from the plants and flowers around you. You are a part of a larger cycle, nurturing these plants as they nurture you. Send love to the flowers in this garden, and all plants and trees in this city for sharing fresh air with you.

Recommendations: 1. Find ad hoc: cafe tucked underground in the West Village and eat lunch surrounded by the eclectic decor. 2. Enjoy lunch at Red Bamboo and try the vegan buffalo wings. 3. Stop by Café Kitsuné for a laptop-free coffee break.

SCIENCES SOCIALE

L'Alliance New York

22 EAST 60TH STREET IN MANHATTAN

(between Madison and Park Avenues)

This French library is a well-kept secret hidden in a historic Beaux-Arts building on the Upper East Side. You must be a member to access it, which means it is rarely crowded. In 1898, the Alliance Française established a chapter in New York, and in 1911, the French Institute was founded. The two organizations later merged to form what is now L'Alliance New York.

Tables are tucked into reading nooks, with warm wooden paneling creating a peaceful atmosphere. The shelves are filled with a wide range of French books, films, music, and educational materials. L'Alliance hosts film screenings, lectures, art exhibits, and language classes throughout the building.

When I was a member, I loved going up to the top floor and taking in the views of the city. As you look out at the thousands of people below, imagine the lives of just a few. As you picture these small vignettes of New Yorkers, remember that each person carries an entire world within them, yet we all coexist here, sharing this city.

Recommendations: 1. Pop downstairs to Café Bibloquet to continue your French excursion with macarons and mouth-watering pastries. 2. Wander into Central Park and walk to the Hallett Nature Sanctuary. 3. Make reservations at The East Pole, a farm-to-table restaurant that serves seasonal meals on the first floor of a brownstone.

The Morgan Library

225 MADISON AVENUE IN MANHATTAN

(between 36th and 37th Streets)

In the heart of Murray Hill lives a literary castle. With stained-glass skylights and towering walnut bookcases, The Morgan Library is often called one of the most beautiful libraries in the world, and for good reason.

Spiral staircases are hidden behind the bookshelves, along with a vintage book elevator once used to move heavy volumes between levels. Originally built in the early 1900s, it holds rare manuscripts, first editions, and works of art from across the centuries.

While most people come for the library, the newly opened garden is just as thoughtfully designed. A pair of marble lions, made by the same sculptor as the New York Public Library lions, guard the entrance. They're surrounded by intricate stone mosaics and a selection of native plants, creating a pristine green space.

Wander among the shelves, surrounded by the beauty of over one hundred thousand books. Each time you step through a doorway into a new room, pause and breathe. These small transitions are invitations to slow down.

Recommendations: 1. See all the giant crystals at Astro Gallery of Gems, Minerals, and Fossils. 2. Get Asian fusion food for dinner at Franchia Vegan Cafe. Try the bibimbap or scallion pancakes. 3. Immerse yourself in the spices of India and the Middle East at Kalustyan's.

Poets House

10 RIVER TERRACE IN MANHATTAN

(between Murray and Vesey Streets)

Discovering little-known libraries has become a superpower of mine, and I was delighted when I stumbled upon Poets House. When you step into the reading room, you are greeted with sweeping views of Rockefeller Park and the Hudson River. The library is airy and light-filled, creating a literary sanctuary in Battery Park City.

This sunny space is home to over seventy thousand volumes of poetry, one of the country's most comprehensive public poetry collections. Founded in 1986 as a donation-based library, Poets House hosts a variety of workshops and literary events, including their annual Poetry Walk across the Brooklyn Bridge, where participants pause at scenic points to read poems aloud together.

Channel your inner writer and craft a short poem. Begin by reading a poem from a nearby book, then write your own version inspired by your personal experience. Focus on the process rather than the outcome, stretching your mind and embracing a creative flow.

Recommendations: 1. Walk along the water and into Teardrop Park to ground yourself in lush greenery. 2. Pick up a coffee at Kaffe Åre and sip it outside at Washington Market Park. 3. Grab a Citi Bike and ride north on the Hudson River Greenway to the Abingdon Square Greenmarket on a Saturday.

Rose Main Reading Room
at the NYPL

476 FIFTH AVENUE IN MANHATTAN
(between 40th and 42nd Streets)

Walking into the Rose Room, you may think you're in the Great Hall of Hogwarts. This grand reading room has fifty-two-foot-high ceilings painted with

murals of pastel pink clouds. Bronze chandeliers hover above the official quiet room in the building, making it a guaranteed space for calm.

The Beaux-Arts building was created after the Astor and Lenox libraries merged to form the New York Public Library in 1895. It opened its doors in 1911, guarded by a pair of marble lions named Patience and Fortitude, which have often been called "New York's most lovable public sculptures."

The Rose Room creates a silent community in Midtown where everyone is in their own world yet peacefully connected. Bring a journal and draw a few symbols to represent what's bringing you joy, whether people, food, or activities. This can be a visual time capsule of this chapter in your life.

1. 6BC Community Garden
2. Alley Pond Environmental Center
3. Amster Yard
4. Brighton Beach
5. Brooklyn Botanic Garden
6. Central Park Conservatory Garden
7. Elevated Acre
8. Governors Island
9. Greenacre Park
10. Hunter's Point South Park
11. Inwood Hill Park
12. Little Island
13. Paley Park
14. Prospect Park
15. Roosevelt Island
16. Snug Harbor Botanical Garden
17. Sutton Place Park
18. Wave Hill

Parks & Gardens

Green spaces are a playground for mindfulness. Become aware of each of your senses. What do you see, hear, smell, touch, and taste as you are surrounded by nature in New York?

6BC Community Garden

630 EAST 6TH STREET IN MANHATTAN

(between Avenues B and C)

The East Village is home to forty community gardens, but 6BC Community Garden is my personal favorite. It has a secret treehouse library in which you can soak in the sunlight and read on a summer afternoon. When I first moved to Manhattan, I lived across the street from the garden, and this lush escape quickly became my respite from the chaos of the city.

Created in the 1980s by a group of volunteers, the garden has since become a publicly preserved green space, beloved by the community. Overflowing with lilacs, irises, tulips, and hundreds of native plants, it offers a blueprint for how nature can thrive in the city. This hidden gem reveals the transformative power of urban green spaces.

As you gaze out from the treehouse window, notice how many shades of green you can see. What looks simply green at first might reveal hints of emerald, olive, or teal. As you leave the garden, carry this sense of curiosity with you into the rest of your day.

Recommendations: 1. Go on a community garden tour through Alphabet City. Start with the 6th Street & Avenue B Community Garden. 2. Sign up for a class at ArtsClub and calm your mind by tapping into your creativity. 3. Sip on a nonalcoholic elixir at Hekate Café & Elixir Lounge.

Alley Pond
Environmental Center

229-10 NORTHERN BOULEVARD IN QUEENS
(between 223rd Street and Cross Island Parkway)

With over 635 acres of ponds, meadows, marshes, hiking trails, and forests, Alley Pond is one of the biggest parks in New York. Its environmental center in

eastern Queens is dedicated to protecting the land and promoting sustainable practices through education and advocacy.

Hidden within the park is the Queens Giant, a 133-foot tulip poplar believed to be the city's tallest and oldest living organism. Standing beside this 350-year-old-plus beauty, I can't imagine a better place to connect with the earth's grounding energy and feel deeply rooted in nature.

As you wander the serene trails, begin to notice the sounds around you. Hear the birds chirping, your footsteps sinking into the marshy earth, and the rustle of wildflowers in the wind. For one full minute, listen closely and pinpoint the faintest sound. Let each note from nature draw you deeper into the present moment.

Amster Yard

211 EAST 49TH STREET IN MANHATTAN

(between Second and Third Avenues)

In the middle of Midtown East, there's a speakeasy-like garden tucked behind a Spanish library. As you walk through the gates of the Instituto Cervantes, you are welcomed into a courtyard surrounded by ivy-covered brick walls. A mirror stands tall at the end of the walkway, giving the illusion that this little pocket of greenery lasts forever.

In the nineteenth century, it was a station on the Boston Post Road, the first postal route in the United States. James Amster purchased it in 1944 and transformed it into the charming courtyard it is today.

This is a well-kept secret I stumbled upon while living in the neighborhood. It quickly became my spot to retreat from the city and have a little meditative moment. As you sit in the garden, notice the textures around you. Look at the delicate ivy climbing the brick walls, the shiny surface of the antique mirror, and the rough pebbles beneath your feet. As you focus on these small details, allow a sense of wonder to wash over you.

Recommendations: 1. Hop on the E or M train to Long Island City and spend the day in Queens. Start with brunch at Cafe Triskell and savor the French toast. 2. Wander to the Windmill Garden, a community garden filled with handmade windmills. 3. Check out what experimental art is on display at MoMA PS1.

Brighton Beach

601 RIEGELMANN BOARDWALK IN BROOKLYN

(between Brighton 6th and 7th Streets)

In the winter, Brighton Beach is one of my favorite places in the city. I am a beach person, but alas, New York has my heart. From where I live, I can get to the ocean in under forty-five minutes, so I started a ritual and go to Brighton Beach once a month. During the off-season, there is barely anyone there, transforming it into a private beach.

The neighborhood, nicknamed "Little Odessa," is primarily Russian and Ukrainian, so you may hear more of those languages than English.

I love walking on the sand from Brighton Beach to Coney Island before hopping on the train home. It is about a thirty-minute walk, just enough time to clear my head as I settle into the serenity of the waves and watch the seagulls soar along the horizon. The stroll from the seaside community at Brighton to the contrasting kitschiness of Coney Island always makes me smile.

As you walk along the water, do a mini beach cleanup. Bring gloves, a trash bag, and pick up ten pieces of litter along the way. As you remove each piece, think about the people who will walk here next, and how your small act of care will help create a cleaner, safer shoreline for them.

Recommendations: 1. Go to Tashkent Supermarket and get the pickled carrots and pierogies for a picnic. 2. Walk 45 minutes to the very end of the beach at Coney Island to catch the sunset. 3. Let the dance of the jellyfish at the New York Aquarium mesmerize you.

Brooklyn Botanic Garden

990 WASHINGTON AVENUE IN BROOKLYN

(between President and Carroll Streets)

During every season, the Brooklyn Botanic Garden is a natural wonderland. In the spring, two hundred cherry blossom trees envelop the Cherry Esplanade. In fall, the foliage transforms the fifty-two acres into shades of orange and red. In winter, you can sip hot chocolate and stroll through the holiday light show. In summer, thousands of roses and wildflowers bloom.

Founded in 1910, the Botanic Garden is dedicated to inspiring an appreciation for the environment through conservation and education. They have transitioned to all-electric landscaping equipment, reducing pollution while creating a quieter, more peaceful experience for both visitors and the surrounding community in Prospect Heights.

One of my favorite spots is the Japanese Garden, with its koi ponds, stone lanterns, and serene Shinto shrine. Find a seat by the reflecting pond and choose a tree to observe. Picture it blooming in spring, lush in summer, orange in fall, and bare in winter. Notice how steady it is through every storm and imagine yourself staying grounded through the changing seasons of your life.

Recommendations: 1. Grab a coffee and breakfast sandwich at Lincoln Station. 2. Try the tapas-like piassa platter with a variety of spiced lentils, greens, and stews at the vegan Ethiopian restaurant Ras Plant Based. 3. Wind down with a candlelit yoga class at Shambhala Yoga.

Central Park Conservatory Garden

1233 FIFTH AVENUE IN MANHATTAN

(between 104th and 105th Streets)

As you step through a giant wrought-iron entrance, you will discover a manicured six-acre formal garden inside Central Park. Divided into three distinct sections, it offers a glimpse into English, French, and Italian botanical design. The English garden features a sculpture honoring Frances Hodgson Burnett, the beloved author of *The Secret Garden.*

Central Park's tree canopy plays a key role in reducing the urban heat island effect, where concrete and other hard surfaces trap heat and raise city temperatures. Green spaces like these act as natural air conditioners, offering shade and helping cool the surrounding area. Even a young tree has a net cooling effect equivalent to ten room-size air conditioners operating for twenty hours a day.

Bring a blanket and find a shady spot to do something rare in the city: lie down for a brief moment. Focus on the sensations around you. Is the air cool on your skin? Is the earth tender beneath you? Embrace the support of the ground as you allow it to fully hold you.

Recommendations: 1. Take a fika (coffee or tea and sweet treat break) at the Church of Sweden. 2. Head to the 82nd Street Greenmarket to pick up fresh produce and pastries on Saturdays. 3. Go to Salon 94 for a minimalist art gallery in a renovated townhouse built in 1915.

Elevated Acre

55 WATER STREET IN MANHATTAN

(between Old Slip and Broad Street)

When you visit this secluded spot, you will not believe you are still in the Financial District. This one-acre park is tucked above the street and offers panoramic views of the East River and the Brooklyn skyline. "Lush" is the last word I would typically use to describe Wall Street, but somehow Elevated Acre evokes that description. Filled with greenery and flowers, it will make you forget you are just steps from the skyscrapers.

In 2005, it was transformed from a previously forgotten elevated deck into a public space. In the summer, there are film screenings in the amphitheater and pop-up markets. Time seems to slow as you are surrounded by blooming flowers and greenery, thoughtfully designed to give you distance from the city.

Watch the clouds travel across the sky. Embody the childlike wonder of imagining what shapes they look like and notice which move faster than others. Then, begin to observe your thoughts like passing clouds. Rather than cling to each one, allow them to drift through your mind with ease.

Recommendations: 1. Walk down to The Battery and visit the colorful SeaGlass Carousel. 2. Have lunch on Stone Street and let the cobblestones transport you back to old New York. 3. Hop on the ferry from Wall Street to the Rockaways and Fort Tilden for a beach day.

Governors Island

FERRY AT 10 SOUTH STREET SLIP IN MANHATTAN
(between Whitehall and Broad Streets)

Hop on a ferry to Governors Island and discover a 172-acre car-free escape. As you wander its verdant paths, it is easy to forget that you are just minutes from Manhattan. A military base for two hundred years, today the island has transformed into a blend of history, art, and sustainability. In the summer, its historic colonial houses are used for artist residencies and filled with immersive installations.

Governors Island has become a playground for climate innovation. The New York Climate Exchange, now under construction, will be a "living laboratory" for sustainable research. The island is already home to urban gardens, beehives, oyster rehabilitation, zero-waste initiatives, and large-scale composting, creating a model for sustainability in cities.

Wander to the Hammock Grove and lay in one of its cocoon-like beds. As hundreds of climate-resilient native plants surround you, listen to the cheerful birdsong. Download a birding app and identify their calls. As you continue walking across the island, keep your ears open and notice how many sounds you now recognize.

Recommendations: 1. Volunteer with the Billion Oyster Project, a nonprofit restoring oyster reefs in New York Harbor. 2. Hop on a Citi Bike and ride around the island's perimeter. 3. Visit the Compost Learning Center to meet the chickens and goats that help make the Zero Waste Island initiative possible.

Greenacre Park

217 EAST 51ST STREET IN MANHATTAN
(between Second and Third Avenues)

Tucked between Midtown skyscrapers is a waterfall so loud that it silences the city. I used to live in the neighborhood, and this tiny park was the first quiet place that sparked the idea for this book. The space is filled with seasonal flowers that bloom around the water, creating a magnetic scene that draws you toward the twenty-five-foot-high waterfall.

The pocket park was built in 1971 thanks to philanthropist Abby Rockefeller Mauzé. It was an early example of how to weave greenery into a dense urban landscape. Inspired by Paley Park, another nearby waterfall park, it became part of a growing movement to create small urban sanctuaries throughout the city.

Sit next to the waterfall and notice the cool mist surrounding you. Focus on the sound of the water rushing and see the texture of the droplets on your skin. Picture a blue bubble surrounding your body, offering calm and protection. Allow yourself to become immersed in a tiny world just seconds from the sidewalk.

Recommendations: 1. Enjoy Indian food, and the lunch special, at Spice Symphony. 2. Have dinner at Copinette and try the truffle risotto. 3. Grab a drink at the Ophelia Lounge and take in gorgeous city views.

Hunter's Point South Park

52-10 CENTER BOULEVARD IN QUEENS

(between 54th and Borden Avenues)

By blending art, nature, and climate resilience, Hunter's Point South Park has become an eleven-acre waterfront oasis. If you walk out on The Overlook, a thirty-foot-high platform hovering over the river, you can see breathtaking views of the Manhattan skyline. If you keep walking south, you will find an art installation called *Luminescence* by Nobuho Nagasawa, which is composed of seven cast concrete domes that represent the phases of the moon.

Once an abandoned post-industrial site, the land has been transformed into a climate-resilient park. One of its most unique features is the tidal marshes, which follow an organic rhythm by flooding gently at high tide and receding at low tide. These marshes help protect the shoreline from storm surges while also creating new habitats for mussels and migratory birds.

Sit on a bench near the water, surrounded by tall grass, and listen to the river against the protected shoreline. As you watch each wave come and go, sync your breathing to its rhythms. Inhale as the water flows in and exhale as it retreats. Notice time slowing down with each passing wave and breath.

Recommendations: 1. Walk north to Gantry State Park to continue a waterside-park day. 2. Bike over the Pulaski Bridge to the Greenpoint Landing Esplanade. 3. Hop on the East River ferry and ride down to DUMBO to walk along the Brooklyn Heights Promenade.

Inwood Hill Park

600 WEST 218TH STREET IN MANHATTAN
(at Indian Road)

At the very top of Manhattan lies one of the most untouched natural parks in the city. Inwood Hill Park spans 196 acres and is home to Manhattan's largest remaining old-growth forest, creating a time capsule of the city's original landscape.

Make sure you wander toward Muscota Marsh, a unique ecological space where fresh water and salt water meet to create a thriving habitat for fish, mollusks, and other aquatic life. The park also holds a deep history, with caves once used by the Lenape people, who lived on this land long before the city was built.

In some parts of the park you can walk without seeing a single building, a rare experience in Manhattan. The park is home to 150 bird species, including bald eagles. Go for a long walk or run, or stretch in the park. Move your body as a way to still your mind. Get a little lost in the winding trails, embracing the disorientation as a way to reconnect with nature.

Recommendations: 1. Continue your nature day by going for a walk in Highbridge Park. 2. Get a farm-to-table brunch at Inwood Farm and try their biscuits. 3. Head to the Bronx and go to the Hall of Fame for Great Americans to see the outdoor sculpture gallery.

Little Island

PIER 55 IN HUDSON RIVER PARK IN MANHATTAN

(between Little West 12th and 13th Streets)

Floating above the Hudson River is a two-and-a-half-acre park. The foundation is made of 132 tulip-shaped concrete columns, creating a new green space over the water filled with winding paths lined with hundreds of flowers and trees. There is even a secret garden with all white roses and birch trees.

Built after Hurricane Sandy damaged Pier 54, Little Island was revitalized by the Hudson River Park Trust. It has become a model for climate resiliency by absorbing storm water, mitigating flooding, and supporting local biodiversity with its native plants.

Sit in the amphitheater to watch the sunset and try a Loving-Kindness meditation. Begin by silently repeating, May I be safe. May I be happy. May I be healthy. May I live with ease. Then extend these wishes to others, like your friends, family, and the people sitting nearby. As the sun reflects on the river, expand your compassion to the entire city.

Recommendations: 1. Grab a bubble tea at Local Roots and walk along Hudson River Park. 2. Take the elevator to the hidden park atop Pier 57 and enjoy incredible views. 3. Get falafel at Miznon and picnic on the beach at Gansevoort Peninsula.

Paley Park

3 EAST 53RD STREET IN MANHATTAN

(between Fifth and Madison Avenues)

Can you believe there are two waterfall parks hidden in Midtown Manhattan? A sister park to Greenacre, Paley Park is a delightful retreat from Fifth Avenue. The twenty-foot-high waterfall blurs out the noise from bustling shoppers, creating a tiny bubble of calm.

One of the first pocket parks in the city, Paley Park opened in 1967 and was funded by William S. Paley, the chairman of CBS. Instead of traditional park benches, it features tables designed by Finnish-American architect Eero Saarinen and chairs by Italian furniture designer Harry Bertoia. It became a model for how tiny, underutilized lots could become urban green spaces.

Surrounded by ivy-covered walls and honey locust trees, you are nestled into a warm hug within the arms of the city. As you gaze into the waterfall, imagine all the places the water has traveled to reach this moment. What oceans and rivers has it passed through? What hidden systems have connected it to this place where it flows freely in front of you? Allow yourself to appreciate all the conditions that have made this beautiful moment possible.

Recommendations: 1. Order a farm-fresh brunch with buttermilk pancakes at 1 Hotel Central Park. 2. Walk down the hidden 6½ Avenue and into the atrium for dinner at La Grande Boucherie's art nouveau space. 3. Wind down with a candlelit yoga class at SonicYoga.

Prospect Park

ENTRANCE AT 20 GRAND ARMY PLAZA IN BROOKLYN

(between Prospect Park West and Flatbush Avenue)

Prospect Park is Brooklyn's only forest, spanning 526 acres of meadows, waterfalls, and woodlands. As you wander toward the wetlands by the boathouse, it becomes serene. I live a block from Prospect Park and think of it as my giant backyard, filled with happy animals and humans alike.

The Prospect Park Alliance has transformed this iconic green space into a more resilient urban forest. By restoring over two hundred acres of natural areas, they have improved water quality, increased biodiversity, and stabilized soil to reduce erosion during heavy storms.

Go to the Vale of Cashmere, a secluded spot away from the main paths. Often called a bird's paradise, it is a marshy haven where hundreds of migrating birds pass through. As you listen to their songs, open a tree identification app and learn the names of three trees around you. Can you spot a weeping cherry tree or a red maple? Knowing their names can deepen our appreciation for the trees that support our city.

Roosevelt Island

TRAMWAY AT 254 EAST 60TH STREET IN MANHATTAN
(between Second and Third Avenues)

Surrounded by panoramic views of the city, yet removed from its frenzy, Roosevelt Island is like a setting in a snow globe. If you hop on the iconic aerial tramway, you'll arrive on a peaceful two-mile stretch of greenery floating between Manhattan and Queens.

The island is now home to the Healing Forest, Manhattan's first pocket forest. This grove is filled with fifteen hundred plants and forty-seven native species. It is a living barrier that prevents flooding, reduces erosion, and filters runoff before it reaches the river.

Roosevelt Island reminds us that calm can exist just one subway stop—or tram ride—from the chaos. Lie down in the grove and practice forest bathing, a Japanese meditation practice of being among nature. One benefit of this practice is that inhaling phytoncides, essential oils released by trees, has been shown to support the immune system. Breathe deeply and observe the trees, taking in the sensory delights around you as you nourish your mind and body.

Snug Harbor Botanical Garden

1000 RICHMOND TERRACE ON STATEN ISLAND

(between Kissel Avenue and Cottage Row)

If you are looking for an escape from Manhattan, hop on the Staten Island Ferry for a peaceful day trip to explore the wetlands and botanical gardens of Snug Harbor. This eighty-three-acre cultural center and green space blends history, horticulture, and environmental advocacy.

I loved learning that Snug Harbor operates a two-and-a-half-acre farm that uses low-till, regenerative practices to care for the soil while providing fresh, local produce to the community. The farm grows over twenty-two thousand pounds of organic vegetables each year through composting, crop rotation, and cover cropping, making it a hidden powerhouse of sustainability within the city.

Bring a film camera or put your phone on Airplane Mode to disconnect. Capture three photos of the gardens through a slower, more intentional lens. As you walk the stone paths of the Chinese Scholar's Garden, notice the way the light hits the koi ponds, the angles of the bamboo groves, or the texture of the waterfall. Rather than taking constant pictures or focusing on the outcome, appreciate the small details of the beauty around you.

Recommendations: 1. Make a reservation at Enoteca Maria to experience the Nonnas of the World, a local restaurant with food cooked by grandmothers from all over the globe. 2. Pack a picnic and wander the reservoir at Silver Lake Park. 3. Hike in Staten Island's Greenbelt at High Rock Park and wander through its ponds and wetlands.

Sutton Place Park

500 EAST 57TH STREET IN MANHATTAN
(between Sutton Place and FDR Drive)

While most waterside parks on the East Side of Manhattan compete with the sound of FDR traffic, Sutton Place Park is uniquely quiet. It is perched above the highway on a raised platform, which muffles the street noise below. The benches overlook the Queensboro Bridge and are surrounded by manicured boxwood hedges and shaded by honey locust trees.

One of the quirkiest parts about this park is the bronze boar. It is a replica of the famous *Il Porcellino* statue from Florence, which philanthropist Hugh Trumbull Adams gifted. To carry on the Italian tradition, just rub the statue's snout for good luck.

Do a progressive muscle relaxation exercise while sitting in the shade. Breathe in as you squeeze the muscles in your face, then exhale and relax them. Slowly move down your body as you tighten your legs, then release. Flex your feet for five seconds, then soften them. Use this awareness to allow any tension to melt away as you rest in this protected grove of trees.

Recommendation: 1. Walk downtown on the East River Esplanade, a greenway with beautiful views of the water. 2. Make a reservation at BODAI Vegetarian, the first Chinese vegetarian restaurant to offer a tasting menu. 3. Go to Tomi Jazz for Japanese food and jazz in a speakeasy-style bar (but be ready to wait on a line).

Wave Hill

4900 INDEPENDENCE AVENUE IN THE BRONX
(between West 249th and 250th Streets)

Hiding in the Bronx is an urban oasis for both humans and hummingbirds. Wave Hill spans twenty-eight acres of lush greenery, blooming flowers, greenhouses, and sweeping views of the Hudson River. Its pollinator-friendly gardens are designed with biodiversity in mind, with thousands of native

plants growing side by side. From monarch butterflies to bumblebees, these little creatures quietly sustain ecosystems that nourish our city.

Originally built in 1843 as a private estate, Wave Hill was once home to famous residents like Theodore Roosevelt and Mark Twain. In 1960, following a suggestion from Robert Moses, the Perkins-Freeman family gifted Wave Hill to the City of New York, transitioning it into a public garden and cultural center.

Walk through the vine-covered pergola overlooking the river and go on a color scavenger hunt. Look for a flower, creature, or small detail in every color of the rainbow. Do you see a red tulip, an orange poppy, a yellow bee? Let this brighten your awareness of the vibrant gardens around you.

1. Green-Wood Cemetery
2. New York Marble Cemetery

Cemeteries

These sacred spaces offer a reminder to appreciate each breath and the gift of being alive. Bring a journal and write down ten things you are grateful for today.

Green-Wood Cemetery

TWENTY-FIFTH STREET AND FIFTH AVENUE IN BROOKLYN

I think Green-Wood Cemetery is the quietest place in Brooklyn. As you walk through the Gothic Revival gates, you enter 478 acres of winding hills, intricate mausoleums, and stunning city views.

This cemetery in South Slope is also a certified arboretum, home to nearly eight thousand trees and an incredible diversity of wildlife. Over two hundred species of birds have been spotted here, including a flock of wild parakeets that nested in the spires above the entrance. The story goes that the birds escaped a shipment at JFK Airport in the 1960s and found a new home in Green-Wood's towers.

Sit by Sylvan Water and look closely at the lake. The water you see today is not the same as it was twenty years ago. The rain, wind, and time have changed it. Now imagine it twenty years from now, filled with different droplets. This body of water reminds us of life's impermanence and invites us to appreciate the ever-changing nature of the world around us.

Recommendations: 1. Pick up a chocolate croissant at Le French Tart and picnic at Green-Wood. 2. Bring a journal and reflect on your day over coffee at Poetica. 3. Grab a vegan breakfast burrito at Roots Cafe and eat at 6/15 Green community garden.

New York Marble Cemetery

41½ SECOND AVENUE IN MANHATTAN
(between 2nd and 3rd Streets)

In the middle of the East Village is a secret cemetery hiding behind a wrought-iron gate. What makes this cemetery so unusual is that there are no visible gravestones. Instead, all the burials are underground, making it look more like a garden than a resting place.

When it was founded in 1830, earth graves were outlawed because of the fear of yellow fever spreading. So, they designed a system of 156 marble vaults, each the size of a small room, buried ten feet belowground.

I first went there for a friend's birthday party. It was a lovely place to picnic and have a contemplative day. (Note: Don't get confused with a similar cemetery one block away, the New York City Marble Cemetery, which is visible from the street.)

Since this space is only open once a month for a few hours, each visit is a rare and sacred experience. Sit on a bench and look up at the sky. Imagine yourself as the sky, not the weather—vast and steady, allowing sunshine and storms to pass while holding space for all that changes.

Recommendations: 1. Get lunch at Divya's Kitchen for a nourishing meal following Ayurvedic principles. 2. Enjoy a plant-based dinner at Ladybird. Try the buffalo maitake bao buns. 3. Have a sauna and cold plunge at the Russian & Turkish Baths.

1. Brooklyn Grange at Sunset Park
2. The Farm at Javits Center
3. Ford Foundation
4. St. Patrick's Cathedral
5. Sylvan Terrace
6. Washington Mews

Buildings

Experiencing awe is a portal to the present moment. Each of these buildings is designed to evoke wonder, inviting you to slow down and appreciate the little details that make them unique.

Brooklyn Grange
at Sunset Park

850 THIRD AVENUE IN BROOKLYN
(between 30th and 32nd Streets)

In Sunset Park, there is a three-acre rooftop farm hidden above the street. Brooklyn Grange grows over eighty thousand pounds of organic vegetables each year and offers a sliding-scale CSA program to make fresh, locally grown produce more accessible.

Green roofs are a symbiotic solution that increase biodiversity, reduce the urban heat island effect, and lower the energy needed to cool the buildings beneath them. During heavy rain, the roof acts like a giant sponge, holding water in the farm beds and slowly releasing it to reduce storm-water runoff and ease pressure on the city's drainage system.

I collaborate with the Brooklyn Grange at their Sunset Park and Brooklyn Navy Yard locations to host watercolor workshops. I love catching a glimpse of the wind turbine across the street at the Balcones Recycling facility.

As you walk through a sea of sunflowers, it is like forest bathing on the roof of an industrial building. Pause beside one flower and imagine everything that helped it bloom: the clouds, rain, sunshine, and farmers who cared for it. An interconnected web of nature forms this single sunflower.

Recommendations: 1. Grab a sandwich for lunch at Tin Cup Cafe. 2. Recharge with a coffee in the backyard of The Black Flamingo. 3. Pick up a sweet treat at Steve's Authentic Key Lime Pie and watch the sunset from the docks in Red Hook.

The Farm at Javits Center

696 WEST 40TH STREET IN MANHATTAN
(between 11th and 12th Avenues)

Just steps above the street, a thriving fruit orchard grows on the roof of New York City's largest convention center. I first discovered the farm at the Javits Center during New York Climate Week and had no idea that a few flights up, a living ecosystem was quietly flourishing.

Brooklyn Grange manages the farm, which produces one hundred thousand pounds of organic produce each year, including leafy greens, arugula, zucchini, cucumbers, and baby carrots. The harvest supports a farm-to-table conference experience for attendees below. The green roof captures over 75 percent of rainfall, preventing seven million gallons of storm-water runoff annually. The farm is a beautiful reminder that even the largest urban buildings can live in harmony with our environment.

Imagine all the little critters keeping this ecosystem in balance. Picture earthworms, fungi, honey bees, and bats working to keep the soil healthy and flowers pollinated. Think about the secret lives of these creatures, each playing an essential role on this farm and in community gardens across the city.

Recommendations: 1. Head to the Drawing Room and use their Art Library to express your creativity. 2. Get gelato at Anita La Mamma del Gelato and savor it in Alice's Garden. 3. Bike south on the Hudson River Greenway to the secret garden at the Church of St. Luke in the Fields.

Ford Foundation

320 EAST 43RD STREET IN MANHATTAN

(between Second Avenue and Tudor City Place)

When I discovered the atrium at the Ford Foundation Building, it was like stumbling upon a hidden rainforest in Midtown. Stepping into the twelve-story enclosed garden is like entering a mini jungle overflowing with ferns, black olive trees, and a pond replenished by rainwater from the roof.

Built in 1967, the building is a glass-and-steel cube supported by concrete and Dakota granite pillars. Inside, landscape architect Dan Kiley designed the first atrium garden in the United States, creating a model for indoor green spaces that blend stunning architecture with nature.

Find the winding path that flows through the atrium and imagine it as a labyrinth for mindful walking. In a city where walking is like a race, slowing down is a radical act. Take each step at half your normal speed, breathing in with each step and out with the next. As you sync your breath to these turtle-like steps, allow your nervous system to settle and embrace the stillness in this secret pocket of peace.

Recommendations: 1. Go on a guided tour of the United Nations and visit the Meditation Room, often called "A Room of Quiet." 2. Hop on the East River ferry and ride to DUMBO for a picnic in Brooklyn Bridge Park. 3. Enjoy the eggplant lasagna—and a candlelit meal—at Coletta, just a short walk south.

St. Patrick's Cathedral

622 FIFTH AVENUE IN MANHATTAN
(between 50th and 51st Streets)

This sanctuary of silence is the largest Gothic Revival cathedral in the United States. Built in 1879, St. Patrick's Cathedral has 330-foot vaulted ceilings and sweeping stained-glass windows that insulate you from the buzz of Fifth Avenue.

While St. Patrick's Cathedral is best known for its stunning architecture, it is also one of the greenest buildings in New York. In 2017, it became home to the largest geothermal project in Manhattan. By drilling twenty-five hundred feet into the earth to access naturally heated water, the cathedral now runs on renewable energy. It has reduced its carbon emissions by 30 percent each year and has become an inspiring example of how even historic landmarks can lead the way in adopting climate solutions.

Sit in the pews and look up at the intricate carvings on the marble columns. From the sculpted panels on the sixteen-thousand-pound bronze doors to the nine-thousand pipes of the Gallery organ, every element of this cathedral is a work of art. As you sit in stillness, enter a state of awe, imagining the craftsmanship that made this building possible.

Recommendations: 1. Try a sensory deprivation tank at FloLo Holistic for the ultimate quiet experience. 2. Have shiitake truffle dumplings at Beyond Sushi. 3. Walk north to the Grolier Club to visit the oldest and largest society for book lovers.

Sylvan Terrace

SYLVAN TERRACE IN MANHATTAN
(between St. Nicholas Avenue and Jumel Terrace)

On this quiet street in Washington Heights, you'll find one of the few places in New York City where wooden homes still stand. Sylvan Terrace is lined with twenty residential rowhouses built in 1882, designed for the middle-class residents who lived on the farmland at the time. The cobblestone street was once the carriage drive leading to the nearby Morris-Jumel Mansion, the oldest house in Manhattan, built in 1765.

Walking through these mews can feel like stepping into the nineteenth century. By the 1970s, many of the homes had been altered, their facades covered in aluminum siding, stucco, and asphalt shingles. In 1979, a federal grant funded their restoration, returning the row to its original uniformity with cream paint, brown trim, and bright green shutters. The houses sit a dozen steps above street level, tucked away just enough that you might miss them unless you knew to look.

Take a step back from the homes and squint your eyes. Notice how the details disappear and you can see just the silhouettes of the buildings and architectural composition. Open your eyes fully and refocus. Appreciate all the intricate detailing you can now observe and feel gratitude for your sight.

Recommendations: 1. Take a tour of the Morris-Jumel Mansion, seeing a piece of history that served as the headquarters for George Washington during the American Revolution. 2. Hop on the bus toward the George Washington Bridge to see the Little Red Lighthouse. 3. Walk around Fort Washington Park and see the Sisyphus Stones, if you're lucky.

Washington Mews

WASHINGTON MEWS IN MANHATTAN

(between University Place and Fifth Avenue)

Behind the gates of this private street in Greenwich Village, you are transported to an earlier era. Tucked just north of Washington Square Park, this one block of ivy-covered buildings is easy to miss.

Built in the 1830s as horse stables, the Washington Mews were later transformed into artist studios. Today, New York University owns the street and uses the colorful buildings for faculty residences and international programs.

I love to come here after walking around Washington Square Park. The contrast between the chaos of the park and the serenity of the mews is a reminder that it is possible to find calm alcoves just steps from the city's busiest places.

Walk on the cobblestones and imagine New York in the 1800s: picture horses and carriages, people in wide-brimmed hats, and a city without cars. Notice how much has changed, while the stones beneath your feet have remained the same.

1. Alice Austen House
2. Bartow-Pell Mansion
3. Earth Room
4. The Guggenheim
5. The Met Cloisters West Terrace
6. The Metropolitan Museum of Art
7. MoMA Sculpture Garden
8. New York Transit Museum
9. The Noguchi Museum
10. Pioneer Works
11. Queens Museum

Museums

Mindful walking is the practice of moving slowly and tuning in to your breath. Museums and galleries are spaces where you can slow down and appreciate the beauty around you.

Alice Austen House

2 HYLAN BOULEVARD ON STATEN ISLAND

(between Bay and Edgewater Streets)

This Victorian Gothic cottage on Staten Island is the historic home of pioneering photographer Alice Austen. She lived here beginning in the 1860s, capturing New York City through more than seven thousand photographs that often documented the lives of immigrants and the working class.

Today, the house serves as a museum and cultural center honoring her legacy, and as a nationally designated site of LGBTQ+ history. It celebrates the fifty-five-year relationship between Alice Austen and her life partner, Gertrude Tate.

Originally built in the early 1690s as a one-room Dutch Colonial farmhouse, the house was purchased by Austen's grandfather in 1844 and expanded into a Victorian Gothic cottage. In the backyard, the grounds have a small private beach with views of the city and the Verrazzano Bridge.

Take a seat on the pebble shoreline and watch the water lap against the earth. Give yourself a Butterfly Hug by crossing your arms over your chest so your hands rest on your shoulders. Begin lightly tapping one side, then the other, in a steady rhythm that matches the waves. Let the movement and repetition calm your nervous system with each beat.

Recommendations: 1. Pick up a sandwich at Montalbano's and eat it at Fort Wadsworth. 2. Go kayaking on the Narrows with Kayak Staten Island. 3. Have authentic Filipino food for dinner at Phil-Am Kusina and try the ube ice cream for dessert.

Bartow-Pell Mansion

895 SHORE ROAD IN THE BRONX
(off Orchard Beach Road)

Nestled within the sprawling Pelham Bay Park, the Bartow-Pell Mansion is a hidden gem in the Bronx. The estate is set on nine acres and includes the Greek Revival mansion, terraced gardens, and a three-story carriage house. The interior is now a museum and filled with vintage decor, gilded chandeliers, and intricate crown molding.

In 1654, Thomas Pell purchased the land from the native Lenape people. In 1888, the estate, including the mansion built by Pell's descendant Robert Bartow, was sold to the City of New York and became part of Pelham Bay Park.

If you want to make a day of it, you can volunteer in their pollinator garden or help care for the herbs and vegetables. Getting your hands in the soil is a calming way to reconnect with the Earth.

Go on a color walk through the gardens by choosing a single color and noticing every bloom or creature in that shade. If you are looking for red, you might spot a poppy, a ladybug, or a cardinal. Focus on the small details, observing the beauty surrounding you.

Recommendations: 1. Walk around Pelham Bay, the city's largest park, and head into the Thomas Pell Wildlife Sanctuary. 2. Soak up more green space and bring a picnic to Seton Falls Park. 3. Spend some time at the New York Botanical Garden. If you go in the winter, make sure you catch the miniature train show.

Earth Room

141 WOOSTER STREET IN MANHATTAN

(between Houston and Prince Streets)

The Earth Room is one of the strangest places in the city, which is exactly why it is one of my favorites. In an apartment building in SoHo, it is filled with 280,000 pounds of dirt. When you walk in, you are both indoors and outdoors at the same time. The earthy scent of soil perfumes this sanctuary of silence.

Created by artist Walter De Maria in 1977, the Earth Room is part of the Dia Art Foundation. Time seems to slow down here, maybe because the installation has been cared for by the same person since 1989. Bill Dilworth, the caretaker, waters and rakes the earth regularly as if it were an apartment-size Zen garden.

There are rarely any other visitors, so you might find yourself alone in the stillness. As you feel a challenging emotion, imagine it flowing out of your body and being absorbed into the soil. Picture the earth composting what you no longer need, transforming it into something new.

Recommendations: 1. Go down the street to see Walter De Maria's complementary installation, *The Broken Kilometer.* 2. Have a delicious Mediterranean brunch at Shuka. 3. Stop by Morgenstern's for ice cream and savor it at the LaGuardia Corner Gardens.

The Guggenheim

1071 FIFTH AVENUE IN MANHATTAN
(between 88th and 89th Streets)

Frank Lloyd Wright designed one of the most iconic buildings in New York, the Solomon R. Guggenheim Museum. It opened in 1959 with an organic spiral architecture inspired by the steep steps of ancient Mesopotamian ziggurats.

The inside gallery features a winding ramp that mirrors the shape of a nautilus shell. Wright subverted the traditional museum layout by having visitors ride to the top and walk down the spiral, passing through interconnected spaces. The museum showcases modern and contemporary art, with a permanent collection that includes works by Kandinsky, Picasso, Chagall, and Mondrian.

One of the quietest spaces in this busy Upper East Side museum is found in the basement. The Aye Simon Reading Room hides behind a keyhole-shaped door. Originally designed as an archive, it was later transformed into a secluded reading space with oak bookshelves and curved tables that mirror the building's design.

As you start at the top, treat the spiral path like a labyrinth for mindful walking. Take each step as slowly as possible, noticing the buzz of foot traffic around you. Imagine you are in a little freeze frame as the world rushes past you.

Recommendations: 1. Pick up a slice of carrot cake at Lloyd's Carrot Cake and eat it in Maggie's Magic Garden. 2. Continue on a museum day and go to the Museum of the City of New York. 3. Wind down at sage + sound for a sound bath or meditation class.

The Met Cloisters
West Terrace

99 MARGARET CORBIN DRIVE IN MANHATTAN
(between Fort Tryon Place and Riverside Drive)

As you wander through stone arches, vaulted ceilings, and lush courtyards, the Met Cloisters transports you to the Middle Ages. Stained-glass windows line the interiors of this branch of the Metropolitan Museum of Art located in Washington Heights.

In 1925, John D. Rockefeller Jr. purchased George Grey Barnard's extensive medieval art collection for the Met. Beginning in 1934, architectural elements from several French monastic cloisters were transported to New York and reconstructed stone by stone to create the museum. Today, the Met Cloisters houses over five thousand medieval works, including the famous Unicorn Tapestries.

With the serene views of Fort Tryon Park and the Hudson River, my favorite place is the West Terrace courtyard. Bring a sketch pad and tap into your inner artist while observing the architecture. Do a blind contour drawing: focus on the building without looking down at your paper. Draw the curves of the arches, the straight lines of the towers, and the rectangle windows. This simple, creative exercise helps you slow down and notice the little details around you.

Recommendations: 1. Stroll through the acres of blooming flowers in Heather Garden. 2. Hike through Fort Tryon Park and enjoy the breathtaking views of the Hudson. 3. Sip on an Ethiopian macchiato at Buunni, where they brew coffee from smallholder farms and farmers' cooperatives.

The Metropolitan Museum of Art

1000 FIFTH AVENUE IN MANHATTAN

(between 80th and 84th Streets)

With its sprawling wings and architectural grandeur, the Met is an iconic stop for New Yorkers and visitors alike. Within its maze-like halls, there are a few surprising pockets of peace. Founded in 1870, the museum holds over two million works of art spanning five thousand years of history.

One of the quietest places is the Astor Chinese Garden Court. Tucked inside the Asian Art galleries on the second floor, you can pass through a moon gate to find a tranquil courtyard filled with koi ponds and bamboo. I like to sit under the skylight and listen to the water feature, embracing an unexpected calm in the busy museum.

Another peaceful escape is the Robert Lehman Collection, where hundreds of paintings from the Italian Renaissance line the walls of the light-filled atrium. Bring a sketchbook and draw with your nondominant hand. Outline the pyramid-shaped atrium, rectangular paintings, and leafy plants. Use this beginner's mindset to invite curiosity and playfulness into your day.

Recommendations: 1. Plan ahead and go to an event at The Explorers Club. 2. Head south to The Frick Collection and the Garden Court on the main floor. 3. Visit the reading room at Cooper Hewitt, Smithsonian Design Museum's library.

MoMA Sculpture Garden

11 WEST 53RD STREET IN MANHATTAN

(between Fifth and Sixth Avenues)

I have visited MoMA many times to experience the incredible modern art inside, but I did not realize a modern oasis was hidden in the museum's backyard. The sculpture garden was designed in 1939 as a space where art, architecture, and nature could coexist.

The garden is filled with groves of birch, beech, and Chinese elm trees that line marble walkways. Fountains and ivy-covered walls calmly insulate you from city sounds. The landscaping is cared for with organic practices, even bringing in little ladybugs to eat aphids on the trees.

Look at the outline of the glass building and imagine drawing a square. Trace up the left side, across the top, down the right, and along the bottom. Now, sync your breath with this pattern. Inhale through your nose for four seconds, then hold your breath for four counts. Exhale through your mouth for four seconds, and hold again for four counts. Repeat this box breathing technique a few times, letting the structure and rhythm anchor your breath and settle your mind.

Recommendations: 1. Hop on the B train to the Upper West Side on a spring day and see hundreds of tulips in bloom at the West Side Community Garden. 2. Relax in The Lotus Garden, a hidden garden on the roof of a parking garage that's only open a few hours a week. 3. Lunch at Peacefood Cafe and try the chickpea fries.

New York Transit Museum

99 SCHERMERHORN STREET IN BROOKLYN

(between Court Street and Boerum Place)

As you walk through the turnstiles of the old Court Street Station, you enter a world of vintage subway cars, historic token machines, and buses from the past century. Once home to a short-lived shuttle to Hoyt-Schermerhorn, the station was decommissioned and transformed into a museum in 1976.

I went to an after-hours swing dance night where we dressed up in flapper outfits and a live band played jazz as people danced on the subway platform. It was a surreal evening that teleported me back to the 1920s.

Go early on a weekday, walk to the end of the platform, and sit on the rattan seats of an empty turquoise train from the 1960s. Known as a "Bluebird," this car was designed in bright blue for the World's Fair. Imagine the people who have sat in this car through the years, while it was in motion and now as a relic. Picture a time-lapse in front of you, a silent film of all the stories this car has witnessed.

Recommendations: 1. Head to One Girl Cookies and have a whoopie pie, an old-fashioned sweet treat. 2. Go thrift shopping at Unearth Vintage, my favorite thrift store in the city. 3. Wind down with an art class or a creative workshop at Brooklyn Renaissance.

The Noguchi Museum

9-01 33RD ROAD IN QUEENS
(between Vernon Boulevard and 10th Street)

Dedicated to the work of Japanese-American sculptor Isamu Noguchi, this museum is a meditative experience. The large-scale stone sculptures invite you to slow down as you move through each airy and minimalist light-filled room.

Housed within a converted 1920s industrial building in Long Island City, the museum reflects Noguchi's values of simplicity, balance, and harmony. He believed in creating "a new nature," one that could exist even within cities.

I like to walk through the sculpture garden, appreciating the thoughtfully designed landscape filled with plants native to Japan and the United States. The contrast between the manicured greenery and bold sculptures is a subtle metaphor for living in balance with nature.

Find a seat by a tree and give yourself permission to do nothing for just a few minutes. Silently tell yourself, I have nothing to do and nowhere to go. Allow this radical act of inaction to settle your mind and body.

Recommendations: 1. Pick up a coffee at Château le Woof and stroll through Socrates Sculpture Park. 2. Go kayaking from Hallett's Cove in the summer. 3. Enjoy brunch at Astoria Provisions and try the huevos rancheros.

Pioneer Works

159 PIONEER STREET IN BROOKLYN

(between Conover and Van Brunt Streets)

Inside a former machine factory in Red Hook, a creative nonprofit arts center now thrives. Once used to build large-scale industrial equipment like railroad tracks and sugar plantation machinery, the space has been reimagined to host exhibitions, artist residencies, and multidisciplinary programs that foster collaboration between artists and scientists.

The backyard garden features a fire pit, an Airstream trailer, and a coffee stand tucked among fruit trees, vegetable beds, and living plant-based installations. The low-lying areas have been landscaped as a salt barrier and sponge to protect against sea level rise. It's even a certified National Wildlife Habitat, providing food and shelter for over 250 species of native plants, birds, and insects.

Sit under the weeping willow tree and try to spot as many animals and critters as you can. Do you see a squirrel, a sparrow, or a bee? New York is home to more than humans, we share the same habitat as so many living beings. Spend the rest of your day imagining the city from a bird's-eye perspective.

Recommendations: 1. Take a bean-to-bar chocolate-making class or take a tour of Raaka Chocolate to learn about single-origin chocolate. 2. Get wood-fired pizza for dinner at Hoek Pizza. 3. Go kayaking with Red Hook Boaters from Louis Valentino Jr. Park and Pier or watch the sun set with views of Manhattan and the Statue of Liberty.

QUEENS MUSEUM

Queens Museum

FLUSHING MEADOWS CORONA PARK IN QUEENS

(between Meridian Road and Avenue of the States)

The Queens Museum is home to one of the most unique exhibits I have ever seen. The Panorama of the City of New York is a wildly detailed miniature version of New York. It is the largest-scale city model in the world and includes every building constructed before 1992.

Created for the 1964 World's Fair by urban planner Robert Moses, the exhibit took three years and one hundred designers to bring to life. I love walking through the exhibit with a bird's-eye view, trying to spot my apartment among the nine hundred thousand tiny buildings that make up this intricate cityscape.

As you step outside the Queens Museum, you are met with the striking sight: the 120-foot-tall Unisphere. Look up and notice the contrast between towering above a miniature city inside and now shrinking beneath a massive globe outside. This rare moment of perspective shares a gentle reminder that our world is part of a much bigger picture.

Recommendations: 1. Enjoy vegetarian Cantonese food and dim sum at Bodhi Village in Flushing. 2. Have some of the best dosas in the city at Hindu Temple Canteen, a cafeteria serving Indian food in the basement of Ganesh Temple. 3. Take a moment of silence as you walk through Cedar Grove Cemetery.

1. 1 Hotel Brooklyn Bridge
2. Book Club Bar
3. Brooklyn Tea
4. Burp Castle
5. Café Regular
6. Caffe Reggio
7. Chai Spot
8. Kettl
9. Ladurée
10. Le Botaniste
11. The Monkey Cup
12. Remi43 Flower & Coffee

Coffee Shops & Restaurants

Mindful eating is the practice of fully savoring each bite of food. As you chew slowly, imagine everyone who helped bring these ingredients to your table. Send gratitude to the farmers, cooks, and servers who have made this meal possible.

1 Hotel Brooklyn Bridge

60 FURMAN STREET IN BROOKLYN
(between Doughty and Vine Streets)

Whether you're treating yourself to a sustainable staycation or vacation, 1 Hotel Brooklyn Bridge offers a nervous system reset. You can start your day by savoring a farm-fresh meal, then take a dip in the rooftop pool with panoramic views of Manhattan and wind down at their spa.

When I visited 1 Hotel Brooklyn Bridge for brunch with a friend, I was drawn to the vertical garden of orchids and succulents. Sustainability is at the heart of this luxury hotel, with the farm-to-table restaurant following low-waste principles, ensuring that surplus food is diverted to local nonprofits. More than half of the hotel was built using regional and reclaimed materials, including tables made from original beams from the Domino Sugar Factory. Even the lobby has a produce stand stocked with imperfect vegetables and fruits rescued from local grocers.

Float on your back in the rooftop pool and let your body become weightless. As tension melts through your fingertips, notice the cool water, warm air, and the color of the sky above. Carry this lightness with you through the rest of your day.

Recommendations: 1. Get delicious plant-based ramen at ippudo V Brooklyn. 2. Grab a matcha at Usagi, a Japanese-inspired art gallery and cafe. 3. Meditate or try an ecstatic dance class at Sound Mind Center.

Book Club Bar

197 EAST 3RD STREET IN MANHATTAN
(between Avenues A and B)

Part bookstore, part bar, Book Club Bar is like a well-loved living room. With a strict no-laptops-after-six-p.m. rule, it is an ideal spot to unplug and relax in the big leather couches beside the fireplace. My ideal night out looks like a night in, and Book Club Bar has mastered that balance.

Book Club Bar has become a community space, hosting a variety of events, including open mic nights, themed book clubs, drawing sessions, and author talks. On sunny days, you can even relax in the backyard patio. Since I don't drink, I love that they offer a nonalcoholic menu alongside their espresso bar, tea, and craft beer selection.

Try a smiling meditation as you sip your tea. Smiling signals to your brain that you're happy, so even if you don't feel joyful at first, it can subtly shift your mood. Silently repeat: Breathing in, I calm my body. Breathing out, I smile to my body. As you leave, offer your barista or fellow book lover a smile, sharing a little joy with the world around you.

Recommendations: 1. Volunteer with the Lower East Side Ecology Center at one of their community gardens. 2. Hop on a Citi Bike and go to Williamsburg for a creative art day at Recess Grove. 3. Have a mindful experience at Reforesters Laboratory for a sound bath and breathwork.

Brooklyn Tea

411 LEWIS AVENUE IN BROOKLYN

(between Decatur and MacDonough Streets)

If you're looking for the best tea in Bed-Stuy, stop by Brooklyn Tea. Founded by Jamila and Ali Wright, this mom-and-pop shop is rooted in their West Indian and Jamaican heritage and built around a mission to connect people through the art and ritual of tea. Partake in a private tea tasting with Ali, a certified tea sommelier, and Jamila as they share the history, science, and steeping methods behind each tea.

You can sit at the tea bar, gather at the communal table, or curl up in the reading nook while enjoying a wide selection of teas and vegan bites. On the wall, you'll even find a sign that reads "wake up and smell the tea," filled with jars of loose-leaf teas for you to try.

Visit the Scent Wall and open the jars one by one. As you lift each lid, take a deep breath and notice the aromas of vanilla rooibos, oolong, or ginger turmeric. Try to identify if it smells sweet, sharp, or earthy. As you close your eyes, allow your focus to become entirely on your sense of smell.

Recommendations: 1. Get a breakfast biscuit at Brown Butter Craft Bar & Kitchen. 2. Stop by Artshack Cafe/Bar for a vegan pastry or even take a ceramics class. 3. Take a yoga class at Noir Yoga, a studio that celebrates diversity, fosters community, and promotes holistic well-being for everyone.

Burp Castle

41 EAST 7TH STREET IN MANHATTAN
(between Second and Third Avenues)

Burp Castle is the only bar in New York that is guaranteed to be quiet. My best friend brought me here for the first time ten years ago, and I was struck by its strangeness. This monastery-themed bar's charm is the bartenders, who hush you if you speak above a whisper.

It is like a beer garden meets a library, an unexpected place to slow down in the East Village. Even on a crowded night, you can still hear your companion talking, unlike every other bar on the block. Instead of blasting loud music, they play ambient Gregorian chants.

The walls are painted with murals of drunken monks, a sentence I never thought I would write. From the name to the experience, everything about this bar is delightfully surreal in the best possible way.

Listen for the bartender to hush the crowd. Treat the request like a mindfulness bell, inviting you to pause. Each time it happens, breathe in deeply and exhale slowly as the room returns to a whisper.

Recommendations: 1. Before heading to Burp Castle, pick up a veggie burger from Superiority Burger and picnic at the 11th Street Community Garden. 2. Have dinner at Spicy Moon, a plant-based Szechuan restaurant. Try the dan dan noodles. 3. Wind down with tea and dessert at Duo Cafe.

Café Regular

158 BERKELEY PLACE IN BROOKLYN

(between Sixth and Seventh Avenues)

With its vintage decor, red leather benches, and tiny space, Café Regular has a charm that's hard to find in New York. The walls are lined with hand-painted murals and antique mirrors, giving the impression that you've stepped into a French film.

The first time I visited Café Regular, I was meeting a friend, and it was so quiet that when I talked I thought I was shouting. When the weather is warm, they have outdoor seating facing the leafy, brownstone-lined street. True to the name, they spotlight regulars on their website, telling stories of locals and building community.

As you sip your coffee, try a 5-4-3-2-1 grounding practice. Start by observing five things you can see, like the lettering on the chalkboard. Then, notice four things you can touch, like your hands on a warm cup. Identify three things you hear, maybe the ambient conversations. Note two things you can smell, like the aroma of sweet croissants. Finally, focus on one thing you can taste, like the bold flavor of espresso. Use this sensory practice to anchor you into the present moment.

Recommendations: 1. Continue on a French cafe crawl and head over to Café Martin. 2. Get gelato at L'Albero Dei Gelati and enjoy it in the GreenSpace at President Street. 3. Have Middle Eastern for dinner at the Zatar Cafe & Bistro.

Caffe Reggio

119 MACDOUGAL STREET IN MANHATTAN

(between West 3rd Street and Minetta Lane)

Caffe Reggio is my most nostalgic spot in the city, a place that brings me back to when I first fell in love with New York at twenty years old. It was the first quiet place my best friend and I discovered while interning in the city. We always hoped to sit at the semicircular table tucked away from the rest of the room, which I later learned is an antique bench that once belonged to the Medici family of Florence.

Caffe Reggio is known as the first cafe in the United States to serve cappuccino. It began as a barber shop in 1927, where the owner offered coffee to clients as they waited. Today, its dimly lit Greenwich Village walls are lined with Italian Renaissance paintings and works from the school of Caravaggio. The original espresso machine still stands proudly, a shimmering relic of the past.

Bring a journal and write about a restaurant or cafe you loved from your childhood. Describe the environment, who you were with, and what food you ate. Bring a smile to your face as you recall all these happy memories and the nostalgia of a place you love.

Chai Spot

156 MOTT STREET IN MANHATTAN

(between Broome and Grand Streets)

I think Chai Spot is the coziest cafe in Manhattan. As you enter, you're invited to remove your shoes and step into the tearoom. There are no chairs, only a sea of endless cushions and colorful pillows for floor seating. You can choose from the nourishing menu of traditional cardamom chai, coconut rose chai, butter chai, or crispy samosas.

This mission-driven cafe promotes peace-building and empowers women and children in Pakistan. Fifty percent of the profits are donated to this goal; they've opened two schools and provide grants to Pakistani women to help them start businesses.

Settle into a cushion and do a body scan. Notice the sensation of your toes touching the rug, your legs on a supportive cushion, and your arms against the pillows. As the cacophony of the city dissipates, appreciate this rare, grounding moment to reconnect with yourself.

Recommendations: 1. Treat yourself to a spa day at AIRE Ancient Baths House in Tribeca. 2. Pick up falafel at taïm and head to the Elizabeth Street Garden for a serene picnic lunch. 3. Hop on a Citi Bike to Greenpoint and go to Hide and Seek for an afternoon tea.

Kettl

70 GREENPOINT AVENUE IN BROOKLYN

(between West and Franklin Streets)

In the middle of Greenpoint, you can sip on matcha sourced from rural farms in Japan. While you wait for your tea to brew, you can watch the stone mill spin slowly, grinding dried green tea leaves into fresh matcha powder. The space is light and airy, a calming backdrop that lets the vibrant green of the matcha shine.

Kettl was founded in 2010 by Zach Mangan and his wife, Minami, who have spent the past decade working to shorten the international supply chain and bring teas from remote regions of Japan to a community around the world. The teas are sourced directly from producers in Japan and often arrive in Brooklyn in less than ten days. Today, they teach hands-on classes that blend whisking and brewing techniques with education on the rich world of Japanese tea.

Order a matcha latte and become curious about its vibrant green color. These tencha leaves are grown in Japan for four years, then shaded for a month to deepen their chlorophyll and flavor. They are handpicked, steamed, cooled, and dried before they arrive in your cup. Imagine the journey each leaf has taken and the beauty held in this single sip.

Recommendations: 1. Walk over to Flower Cat and enjoy a refreshing hibiscus lemonade. Pick up a bouquet of fresh flowers for yourself or a loved one. 2. Plan a tour of Kingsland Wildflower Green Roof and watch the sun set over the city skyline. 3. Take a wheel-throwing class at Yaro and craft a teacup for the matcha you bring home.

LADUREE

Ladurée

398 WEST BROADWAY IN MANHATTAN
(between Spring and Broome Streets)

A sweet piece of Paris sits in the heart of SoHo. Ladurée, the iconic French patisserie, brings a taste of Europe to New York with its pastel decor, delicate teacups, and ornate furnishings. This location opened in early 2014 as the brand's first full-service restaurant in the United States.

You enter by passing the display case filled with rainbow rows of macarons. As you pass through the Pompadour Room, which feels like stepping into the world of Marie Antoinette, you will find an idyllic backyard garden. Tucked away from the busy street, you can experience a full tea service beneath blooming cherry blossom trees in the spring or vibrant foliage in the fall. Reservations go quickly during peak season in the spring, so make sure you plan ahead to dine in this serene spot.

Order one of the signature macarons like black currant, passion fruit, or salted caramel. Take a moment to notice its textures as you eat it: crisp on the outside, with a sweet, chewy ganache center. Slow down for a single bite, and savor the simple delight of this small treat.

Recommendations: 1. Walk over to The Climate Museum, the first museum dedicated to climate in the United States. 2. Take a sound-bath yoga class at Sui Yoga & Spa Thermae, or just stop in for a snack at their cafe. 3. Stop by Raffetto's to pick up fresh pasta to make for dinner.

Le Botaniste

156 COLUMBUS AVENUE IN MANHATTAN
(between 66th and 67th Streets)

Fast-casual has never been so nourishing. Walking into Le Botaniste is like stepping into a nineteenth-century French apothecary, complete with antique pharmacy bottles, vintage labels, and white marble counters. The checkered floors and wooden accents add to its charm, creating a serene space to enjoy a balanced, beautifully plated meal.

The menu has "botanical prescriptions," because each dish is plant-based and organic, designed to support the health of your body and the planet. It was the city's first carbon-neutral restaurant and shares each meal's carbon footprint on its website.

Even my non-vegetarian friends love it, delighted by the creative flavors and chic ambiance. In winter, I order the mushroom stroganoff from their seasonal menu to warm up on a chilly day.

As you eat your meal, take one bite at a time. Rest your utensil on the table between bites, noticing any natural urge to rush. Finish chewing fully before eating more. Let this slow rhythm help you savor the deliciousness of the food.

Recommendations: 1. Visit the original location of Levain, on the Upper West Side, for a chocolate chip walnut cookie. 2. Check out Septuagesimo Uno, one of the city's smallest parks. 3. Walk south along the West Side waterfront.

The Monkey Cup

1965 ADAM CLAYTON POWELL JR. BOULEVARD IN MANHATTAN

(between 118th and 119th Streets)

This jungle-themed cafe is a beloved neighborhood favorite in Harlem. Owned by Laura and Alfredo, a couple from Venezuela, they've created a welcoming space to go offline and sip delicious coffee.

Alfredo, a classical musician, dreamed of opening a cafe that would be both affordable and inviting to fellow artists and musicians. The shop is named after his childhood nickname, Monkey, and its design is inspired by the rainforests of Venezuela. Everything in the space was built from scratch, from the tree-shaped bookshelf that Alfredo learned woodworking to create to the faux-ivy ceiling designed by Laura.

The shop doesn't offer Wi-Fi, instead encouraging you to slow down, read from the tree library, or connect with a friend. You can also enjoy Venezuelan-inspired snacks like fresh arepas while you relax at the handmade communal table.

Bring a coloring book to the coffee shop and doodle in the pages. You don't need to be an expert artist to enjoy the meditative process of coloring. Making art, even doodling, can reduce stress, help process emotions, and improve focus.

Recommendations: 1. Grab ice cream at Sugar Hill Creamery and eat it at the top of Marcus Garvey Park by the old fire tower. 2. Get lunch at Dear Mama Cafe and then walk down Riverside Park to the Cathedral of St. John the Divine. 3. Have dinner at Winnie Said and try Micah's Mac and Cheese.

Remi43 Flower & Coffee

810 SECOND AVENUE IN MANHATTAN

(between 43rd and 44th Streets)

With palm trees and pothos plants surrounding wooden tables, Remi43 resembles a tropical greenhouse in Midtown Manhattan. The store sells floral arrangements and orchids, alongside coffee and pastries. As you walk up the winding staircase to the tucked-away second floor, you can look out over a field of fiddle leaf figs and snake plants. Founded in 2017 by Remi Kim, the idea for this duo-concept store was inspired by her time studying in South Korea.

Greenery enhances mental well-being by reducing stress and lifting our mood. A plant-and-flower-filled cafe like this one, which incorporates nature in an unexpected setting, provides a serotonin boost.

As you relax beside the plants, observe a single orchid. Notice how many colors are in one petal, where it connects to the stem, and the smallest details you can find. This simple act can help you appreciate and build awareness of the hidden beauty that surrounds you.

Recommendations: 1. Get lunch at Little Collins and order shakshuka. 2. Walk over to Tudor City Greens, an elevated park across the street from the United Nations. 3. Pick up fresh produce at the Dag Hammarskjold Greenmarket on Wednesdays.

1. Happy Medium
2. Open Care Community
3. Othership
4. QC Spa
5. Three Jewels
6. Vessel Floats

Activities

In a city that never sleeps, it is easy to become exhausted. These activities will help you reconnect with yourself and find a community of others who value calm.

Happy Medium

49 MARKET STREET IN MANHATTAN
(between Madison and Monroe Streets)

When you walk into Happy Medium, you are cocooned in a warm, candlelit cafe. But instead of food you order off the art menu: you can watercolor, paint ceramics, collage, and use oil pastels. It is a welcoming space to tap into your creativity without needing to be an artist.

I attended a session with a group of friends and had one of my favorite New York days ever. I organized a Pancakes and Paint event, where we did pottery painting at Happy Medium and then went across the street for the best pancakes at Golden Diner. I can't recommend this combo enough.

Take a wheel-throwing class in the downstairs studio and allow yourself to play with clay. Notice how the clay is slippery between your fingers or smooth as you mold it. Get your hands messy and focus on the process of creating rather than the outcome. Making art with your hands allows you to step out of your head and return to your body.

Recommendations: 1. Try vegan dim sum at Bodhi Vegetarian Restaurant in Chinatown. 2. Go to Jajaja Mexicana and get the churritos with coconut dulce de leche for dessert. 3. Stop by Mmuseumm, the smallest museum in the city, to see its rotating tiny exhibits (open weekends only).

Open Care Community

44 COURT STREET IN BROOKLYN

(between Joralemon and Remsen Streets)

Community acupuncture is one of the quietest group activities I've experienced. Open Care Community offers sliding-scale prices during their community acupuncture sessions, creating an accessible self-care option for all income levels.

I never thought I would find acupuncture calming, but it has been one of the most pleasant surprises of my year. Somehow, lying with needles in my back is a strangely meditative experience. It's a rare time that I can't go anywhere or do anything for twenty minutes. After the session, it feels as if I've taken a restful nap and recharged my battery.

Slow your breath as they gently place the thin needles. It's okay to feel the discomfort, just trust that it will pass quickly. This ancient form of traditional Chinese medicine has been practiced for thousands of years. Each placement supports healing and helps restore balance in your nervous system. At this moment, your only job is to rest.

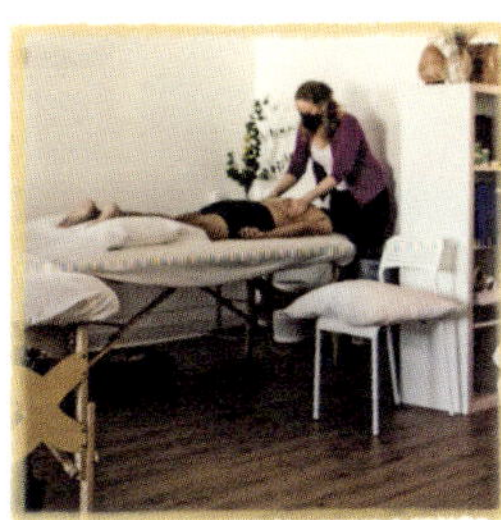

Recommendations: 1. Stop by Sahadi's to pick up fresh Middle Eastern spices and try the pistachio baklava.
2. Get a banana and Nutella crepe at The Little Sweet Café.
3. Have a farm-to-table Northern Italian dinner at Rucola.

Othership

25 KENT AVENUE IN BROOKLYN

(between North 12th and North 13th Streets)

Nothing makes time stand still like being submerged in a thirty-two-degree ice bath. Othership, a sauna and cold plunge spa in Williamsburg, is designed to awaken your senses. Their guided sessions blend meditation, breathwork in the sauna, and a cold plunge.

My favorite part is when the guides place snowballs filled with essential oils onto the hot stones, and the scent of cedarwood, eucalyptus, or clove drifts through the air. After twenty sweaty minutes in the sauna, jumping in ice-cold water doesn't sound too bad. I do my best to slow my breath, letting the cold reset my nervous system. I can barely last thirty seconds, but I always feel proud for stepping outside my comfort zone.

As you enter the water, lean into the intensity of the cold. As you notice the tingling and discomfort, focus on your breath by inhaling and exhaling slowly. Stay with it for just a few more seconds, then step out. As you sit on the bench, feel your body enter a new state of aliveness.

Recommendations: 1. Plan ahead and volunteer at the McCarren Park Demonstration Garden. 2. Slow down with a creative class at Recess Grove. Learn how to do linocut printmaking in their studio or about plant propagation in their garden. 3. Pick up a snack and cute stationery at Loaf on Paper.

Reading Rhythms

READINGRHYTHMS.CO

Walking into a Reading Rhythms event is like reading in a living room with new friends. The signature program starts with one hour of reading and ends with time to reflect with fellow bookworms. When I went to my first Reading Rhythms event, it was in the back of a candlelit bar, and they had a pianist playing live instrumental music.

The motto is "Not a book club. A reading party." The parties are held in both iconic venues and intimate local spaces, always with a peaceful ambiance. It is a unique way to disconnect from your phone, relax into the present moment, and leave the evening refreshed.

Bring a book and get lost in the story. There is something special about slipping into your own world while still connected to the calming presence of others around you.

Recommendations: 1. Spend a reflective evening with Emily from @journalingclasses during one of the Jazz & Journaling nights. 2. Take a craft therapy workshop at art gurl to unwind through creativity. 3. Attend a Creative Morning Club meetup and explore a new art-related hobby.

READING
RHYTHMS

QC Spa

112 ANDES ROAD ON GOVERNORS ISLAND

I'm a big fan of bathhouses, and QC Spa takes the cake. Once a military post on Governors Island, it has been transformed into a three-story luxury spa with outdoor pools, saunas, cold plunges, steam rooms, and sensory showers.

I celebrated my birthday here, wrapped in a robe while reading alongside friends and bathing in the infinity pool with views of Manhattan. One of the most memorable experiences was floating in a warm outdoor pool and listening to soothing music that could only be heard underwater.

Go into the sauna for ten minutes and then into the ice room, mimicking a cold plunge as you feel your body come alive. Time slows down as you rotate between Vichy showers and foot baths, cocooned by the candlelit stone walls. It is a peaceful retreat that seems far from the city, though just a ferry ride away.

Three Jewels

5 EAST 3RD STREET IN MANHATTAN
(between Bowery and Second Avenue)

This airy yoga studio provides a sanctuary to reflect and reset, even on the busiest days. With the city moving quickly outside, Three Jewels is a space to pause through stilling your mind and body.

This is a "modern-day urban dharma center" and teachers share ancient Buddhist philosophy with practical tools for daily living. They offer yoga and meditation classes upstairs and have a cafe with teas and plant-based snacks downstairs.

During class, thank your body for its strength and the way it supports you. Let gratitude wash over you as you feel it stretch and move. Carry that same appreciation as you leave, remembering the gift of simply being present in your body.

Recommendations: 1. Buy fresh fruit at the Tompkins Square Greenmarket on a Sunday to eat mindfully before a meditation class. 2. Try the vegan burrito at Spring Cafe Aspen. 3. Recharge with a smoothie at the Moroccan inspired Pause Cafe.

Vessel Floats

101 WEST STREET IN BROOKLYN

(between Kent Street and Greenpoint Avenue)

The quietest place in New York might be inside a sensory deprivation tank in Greenpoint. These float tanks are filled with two thousand pounds of salt water, an even higher salt content than the Dead Sea, to make floating feel effortless.

The tanks are soundproof and block out any light, creating an immersive experience. By eliminating sensory overload, it allows your brain to enter a theta-state, which feels like being between half-awake and half-dreaming. This theta state can help to reduce anxiety and lower cortisol levels.

Vessel's tanks are unique because, rather than the traditional floating pod that might make you feel claustrophobic, these are like a large private bathtub with high ceilings. You enter by opening a portal-like door, finding a tank illuminated by purple lighting when you enter. The light turns off when you start floating, creating total darkness. The experience isn't for everyone, but I enjoyed trying it and embracing the fully weightless sensation.

As you float in the salt water, feel supported by the it. Outside, you have to exert energy to walk, but right now you don't need to use any energy. Allow your mind to drift into a theta state.

Recommendations: 1. Have lunch in the backyard of Cafe Alula and try the cauliflower "shawarma." 2. Grab a book and take it to the rooftop of the Greenpoint Library in the outdoor reading area. 3. Enjoy Thai home cooking at Little Tiffin and try the khao soi.

Recommendations by Neighborhood

This list of all of the recommended places in the book is organized by neighborhood to make planning day trips easier. You can view the full map of locations on Google Maps at QuietestPlaces.com.

THE BRONX

Bartow-Pell Mansion
New York Botanical Garden
Pelham Bay Park
Seton Falls Park
Thomas Pell Wildlife Sanctuary
Wave Hill

BROOKLYN

Bed-Stuy

Artshack Cafe/Bar
Brooklyn Tea
Brown Butter Craft Bar & Kitchen
Noir Yoga

Brighton Beach & Coney Island

Brighton Beach
End of the beach at Coney Island
New York Aquarium
Tashkent Supermarket

Brooklyn Heights & DUMBO

1 Hotel Brooklyn Bridge
Brooklyn Bridge Park
Brooklyn Heights Promenade
Center for Brooklyn History
ippudo V Brooklyn
One Girl Cookies
Sound Mind Center
Usagi

Carroll Gardens & Cobble Hill

Brooklyn Poets
Liz's Book Bar
Mazzola
Saturn Road
The Secret Garden Brooklyn
Unearth Vintage

Downtown Brooklyn & Fort Greene

Brooklyn Renaissance
The Center for Fiction
Fort Greene Park Greenmarket
Greenlight Bookstore
Library for Arts and Culture
The Little Sweet Café
New York Transit Museum
Open Care Community
Rucola
Sahadi's

Greenpoint & Williamsburg

Cafe Alula
Flower Cat
Greenpoint Landing Esplanade
Greenpoint Library Rooftop
Hide and Seek
Kettl
Kingsland Wildflower Green Roof
Little Tiffin
Loaf on Paper
McCarren Park Demonstration Garden
Othership
Recess Grove
Reforesters Laboratory
Vessel Floats
Yaro

Park Slope & South Slope

6/15 Green community garden
Café Martin
Café Regular
Community Bookstore
Electric Beets
GreenSpace at President Street
Green-Wood Cemetery
L'Albero Dei Gelati
Le French Tart
Poetica Coffee
Roots Cafe
Un Posto Italiano

The Met Cloisters West Terrace

The Monkey Cup

Morris-Jumel Mansion

Sisyphus Stones

Sylvan Terrace

Lower East Side & SoHo

Angel Orensanz Foundation

Bodhi Vegetarian

The Broken Kilometer

Chai Spot

The Climate Museum

Earth Room

Happy Medium

Housing Works Bookstore

Hudson River Park

Jajaja Mexican

Ladurée

LaGuardia Corner Gardens

LuAnne's Wild Ginger

Mmuseumm

Morgenstern's

Raffetto's

Shuka

Sui Yoga & Spa Thermae

Midtown & Midtown East

1 Hotel Central Park

6½ Avenue

Amster Yard

Beyond Sushi

BODAI Vegetarian

Coletta

Copinette

Dag Hammarskjold Greenmarket

East River Esplanade

FloLo Holistic

Ford Foundation

Greenacre Park

Grolier Club

La Grande Boucherie

Little Collins

MoMA Sculpture Garden

Ophelia Lounge

Paley Park

Remi43 Flower & Coffee

Rose Main Reading Room at the NYPL

SonicYoga

Spice Symphony

St. Patrick's Cathedral

Sutton Place Park

Tomi Jazz

Tudor City Greens

United Nations Meditation Room

Murray Hill

Astro Gallery of Gems, Minerals, and Fossils

Franchia Vegan Cafe

Kalustyan's

The Morgan Library

Roosevelt Island

Upper East Side

82nd Street Greenmarket

Albertine

Café Bibloquet

Central Park Boathouse

Central Park Conservatory Garden

Church of Sweden

Cooper Hewitt, Smithsonian Design Museum Library

The East Pole

The Explorers Club

Florence Gould Garden

The Frick Collection

The Guggenheim

Hallett Nature Sanctuary

Isle of Us

L'Alliance New York

The Metropolitan Museum of Art

Museum of the City of New York

sage + sound

Salon 94

Upper West Side

Le Botaniste

Levain

The Lotus Garden

Peacefood Cafe

Septuagesimo Uno

West Side Community Garden

West Side waterfront

QUEENS

Douglaston

Alley Pond Environmental Center

Flushing

Bodhi Village

Cedar Grove Cemetery

Hindu Temple Canteen

Queens Museum

Long Island City

Astoria Provisions

Cafe Triskell

Château le Woof

Gantry State Park
Hallett's Cove
Hunter's Point South Park
MoMA PS1
The Noguchi Museum
Socrates Sculpture Park
Windmill Garden

Rockaways

Fort Tilden

STATEN ISLAND

Alice Austen House
Enoteca Maria
Fort Wadsworth
High Rock Park
Kayak Staten Island
Montalbano's
Phil-Am Kusina
Silver Lake Park
Snug Harbor Botanical Garden
Staten Island's Greenbelt

GOVERNORS ISLAND

Billion Oyster Project
Compost Learning Center
QC Spa

CITY-WIDE ACTIVITIES

@journalingclasses with Emily
art gurl
CreativeMorning Clubs
Reading Rhythms

Photo Credits

p. 8: Esra Karakose Balioglu
pp. 11, 13, 17, 20, 23, 32, 36, 40, 47, 49, 57, 65, 76, 80, 105, 121, 123, 126, 133, 143: Nicole Kelner
p. 15: The Center for Fiction/Michelle Rose Photography
p. 19: Marginalmonkeys
p. 24: Paolatrabanco
p. 27: Poets House
p. 39: King of Hearts
p. 43: Bill B
pp. 45, 70: Rhododendrites
p. 51: Daniel J. Prostak
p. 53: The rakish fellow
p. 54: Praneeth Thalla
p. 63: Jim.henderson
p. 73: Caroline S. DuBois
p. 79: Ajay Suresh
p. 83: Peter K Burian
p. 85: Beyond My Ken
p. 91: Jordon Briggs
p. 93: Swizz152
p. 94: 19h00s
p. 97: Wallyva
p. 99: The Metropolitan Museum of Art
p. 101: Thomson200
p. 103: Velvet
p. 107: Nicholas Knight © The Isamu Noguchi Foundation and Garden Museum, New York: Artists Rights Society
p. 109: Taylornelson
p. 111: OptimumPx
p. 114: Opencooper
p. 117: Elle Kenwood
p. 119: Brooklyn tea
p. 129: Kettl
p. 131: The Integer Club
p. 134: The Monkey Cup
p. 137: Remi43
p. 141: Jacey Adler
p. 145: Othership
p. 146: Reading Rhythms
p. 151: Three Jewels
p. 152: Vessel Floats

Acknowledgments

New York has been the backdrop of my favorite memories. When I was little, my parents brought me on day trips from our tiny town to visit the big city. In college, I met my best friend in NYU summer housing. And today, I've become an artist with a studio in DUMBO, shared with three incredible studio mates. I am grateful to so many people for helping me explore this city and now turn my chaotic Google Maps stars into a constellation of quiet places that I could share with you.

Look, Mom, I wrote a book! Mom and Dad, I am so lucky to be your daughter. Thank you for always encouraging my creativity and believing in my big ideas. I love you so much.

New York is where I've met my best friends. They've been my adventure buddies through so many of these strange and beautiful places. Abi, you helped me see this city with wonder when we were little baby interns. I can't imagine New York without you. Melina, there's nothing better than adding stamps to my memory passport with you.

To my studio mates, Johna, Liz, and Skye, thank you for your incredible feedback on all my painting days. You have made me a better artist. And to my art friends, especially Alice, thank you for your constant inspiration and encouragement.

To my friends and family who have been there for me during the hard times, thank you for cheering me on and making the fun times even more special.

I am forever grateful to my publisher, Jim Muschett, for reading my Substack and seeing the potential for this book. Thank you to the entire Rizzoli team, especially my editor, Tricia Levi, and designer, Tanya Ross-Hughes, for bringing it to life with such care.

To my amazing agent, Laurie Abkemeier, thank you for guiding me through creating my first book. I am grateful for your incredible feedback and insight during every step of this process.

Thank you to Thich Nhat Hanh and the Plum Village community. Their teachings have shaped many of the mindfulness practices throughout these pages.

To Jaime Banks and Trish Glass from Quiet Communities, thank you for helping me connect the dots between quiet and climate change.

I honor the Lenape, Canarsie, and Wappinger peoples, the original stewards of the land we now call New York City. This book was created on Lenapehoking, their ancestral and unceded homeland.

Thank you to my climate community for showing me it's possible to imagine and build the world we want to live in. You helped me discover New York through the often-invisible lens of climate resiliency.

And to everyone who has read or shared my art online, your support made this book possible.

I am endlessly grateful to the humans, maple trees, park benches, and pigeons that make New York, New York.

About the Author

NICOLE KELNER is an artist and climate communicator living in Brooklyn, New York. She creates educational art about climate change solutions and has worked with the U.S. Department of Energy, Harvard, *The Guardian*, and New York University. Her work has been featured in *Forbes*, *The Washington Post*, and *The Verge*. She is the author of *Electrify Everything: The Clean Energy Coloring Book* and *A Brighter Future: Illustrating Climate Change and Solutions*. Learn more at nicolekelner.com and follow her on Instagram at @mindfulnicole.

You can never step in the same river twice. Both you and the river have changed. The same goes for New York. The city is ever-evolving, just like you. Make sure to check the hours before visiting these quiet places, as they may have changed since I wrote this.

First published in the United States of America in 2026 by
Rizzoli Universe,
A Division of
Rizzoli International Publications, Inc.
49 West 27th Street
New York, NY 10001
www.rizzoliusa.com

Publisher: Charles Miers
Associate Publisher: James Muschett
Editor: Tricia Levi
Design: Tanya Ross-Hughes
Managing Editor: Lynn Scrabis

ISBN: 978-0-7893-4627-8
Library of Congress Control Number: 2025946082

Printed in China

2026 2027 2028 2029 / 10 9 8 7 6 5 4 3 2 1

The authorized representative in the EU for product safety and compliance is Mondadori Libri S.p.A., via Gian Battista Vico 42, Milan, Italy, 20123, www.mondadori.it

Visit us online:
Instagram: @RizzoliBooks
Facebook.com/RizzoliNewYork
Youtube.com/user/RizzoliNY

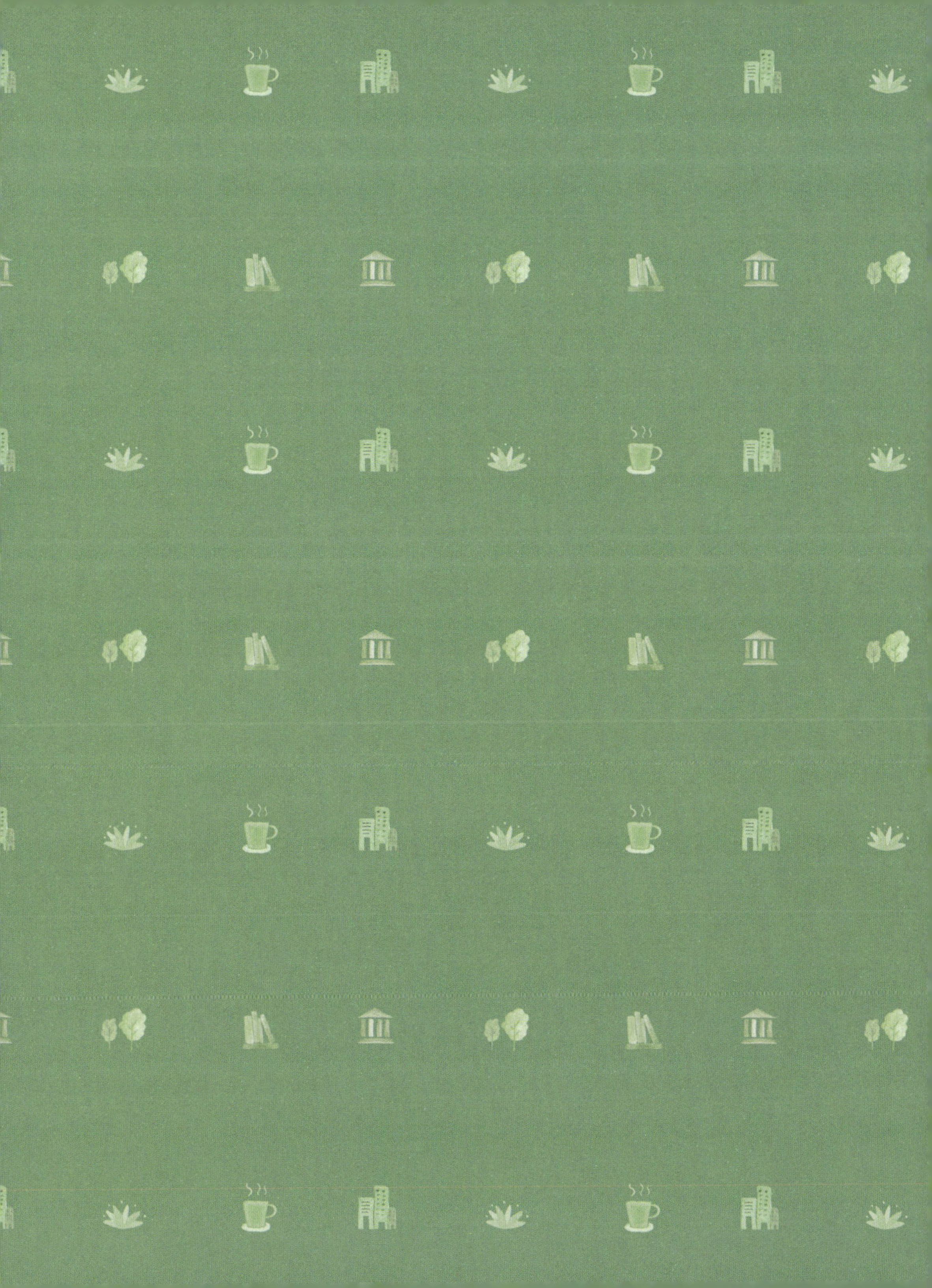